irish saints

BOOKS BY ROBERT T. REILLY

IRISH saints

BY ROBERT T. REILLY

ILLUSTRATED BY HARRY BARTON

WINGS BOOKS
NEW YORK • AVENEL, NEW JERSEY

This edition is published by Wings Books,
distributed by Outlet Book Company, Inc.,
a Random House Company,
40 Engelhard Avenue, Avenel, New Jersey 07001,
by arrangement with Farrar, Straus & Giroux, Inc.

Random House
New York • Toronto • London • Sydney • Auckland

Manufactured in the U.S.A.

Library of Congress Cataloging-in-Publication Data

Reilly, Robert T.
    Irish saints / by Robert T. Reilly : illustrated by Harry Barton.
        p.   cm.
    Originally published : New York : Avenel Books, 1964.
    Summary: Brief lives of canonized saints and other good people
from Irish History, including St. Patrick and St. Brigid, as well as
Matt Talbot and Bishop Galvon.
    ISBN 0-517-36833-1
    1. Christian saints—Ireland—Biography—Juvenile literature.
[1. Saints. 2. Christian biography. 3.Ireland—Biography.]
I. Barton, Harry, ill.   II. Title.
[BX4659.I7R4   1992]
282'.092'2415—dc20
    [B]   92-26028

CIP
                                                              AC

10 9 8 7 6 5 4

NIHIL OBSTAT:

    Rev. William F. Hogan, S.T.D.
        Censor Librorum

IMPRIMATUR:

    ✠ Most Reverend Thomas A. Boland, S.T.D.
        Archbishop of Newark

contents

The Irish saints whose stories are told in this book are "saints" in the broad religious sense. Some have been canonized by the Church; others, though not formally saints, are nonetheless saintly and may one day be added to the Church's roster of the canonized.

fOREWORD

From the Bog of Allen in Offaly, the Boyne
River flows northeast across the limestone plain
and empties into the Irish Sea twenty miles above
Dublin. Midway in its course it glides past the
green hill of Tara where, in ancient times, the
High Kings of Ireland lived and ruled.

On a night more than 1500 years ago, the
sun set on this darkened mound, stretching its
shadow across the valley grasses, finally cloaking
stream and sky and plain. It was the eve of King
Leary's birthday, and royal decree commanded
that no fires be lit until the High King's Druids
kindled the festive blaze on Tara's heights.

Suddenly, across the river, a flame leapt sky-
ward from the Hill of Slane. King Leary summoned his pagan priests and demanded to know
the source of this outrage.

They responded slowly, mysteriously.

"Unless yonder fire be extinguished this night,
it will burn forever. It will outshine all fires that
we light. And he who lit it will conquer us all
and rule over this island from henceforth."

Angrily, the High King dispatched thirty

chariots to the distant hill with orders to smother the blaze and capture the transgressor.

Patrick heard them coming in the night, the horses panting up the slope, the armor creaking. Before his tent the fire burned, for this was also the eve of Easter and this was his Paschal flame. His few companions gathered about him. Patrick comforted them.

"Let them that will, trust in horses and chariots," he said, "but we walk in the name of the Lord."

Soon Patrick's camp was overrun and he and his followers taken. But the soldiers could not quench the fire. They commanded the missionaries to march to Tara.

It was now Easter morning, and, as the little band processed toward the court of King Leary, they chanted the sacred *Lorica*, a prayer composed by Patrick for their protection:

"I arise today
 Through the strength of heaven:
 Light of sun,
 Radiance of moon,
 Splendor of fire,
 Speed of lightning,
 Swiftness of wind,
 Depth of sea,
 Stability of earth,
 Firmness of rock.

I arise today
Through God's strength to pilot me:
God's might to uphold me,
God's wisdom to guide me,
God's eye to look before me,
God's ear to hear me,
God's word to speak for me,
God's hand to guard me,
God's way to lie before me,
God's shield to protect me,
God's host to save me
From snares of devils,
From temptation of vices,
From everyone who wishes me ill
Afar and anear
Alone and in a multitude.

I summon today all these powers between me and
    those evils:
Against every cruel merciless power that may oppose
    my body and soul;
Against incantations of false prophets,
Against black laws of Pagandom,
Against false laws of heretics,
Against craft of idolatry,
Against spells of women and smiths and wizards,
Against every knowledge that corrupts man's body
    and soul.

Christ to shield me today
Against poison, against burning,
Against drowning, against wounding,
So that there may come to me abundance of reward.

Christ with me, Christ before me, Christ behind me,
Christ in me, Christ beneath me, Christ above me,
Christ on my right hand, Christ on my left,
Christ when I lie down, Christ when I sit down,
    Christ when I arise,
Christ in the heart of every man who thinks of me,
Christ in the mouth of everyone who speaks of me,
Christ in every eye that sees me,
Christ in every ear that hears me.

I arise today through a mighty strength,
The invocation of the Trinity:
Through belief in the Threeness,
Through confession of the Oneness
Of the Creator of Creation."

Reciting this litany, they crossed the soft pastures of clover and ascended the pagan mound of Tara. Doing so, they marched into history.

We know now that there were missionaries in Ireland before Patrick and Christians before his disciples. His advent, however, marked the real beginning of that constant faith which was prophesied by the Druids. Holy men and women followed him—scholars, martyrs, wanderers, ascetics, reformers. Finally the faith came full circle and Ireland sent forth missionaries of its own to Christianize other pagan lands. Some were saints and some were merely saintly. All walked in the footsteps of Patrick who stirred the dust of kings that Easter morning. All came under his protection and shared his benediction:

"Christ with me, Christ before me, Christ behind me, Christ in me, Christ beneath me, Christ above me, Christ on my right hand, Christ on my left. . . ."

This is their story.

irish saints

(418?-493?) st. patrick

CHAPTER ONE

"I arise today through the strength of heaven . . ."

At the beginning of the fifth century, the hopes
for Christianity in Ireland rested upon the slim
shoulders of a sixteen-year-old slave. His name
was Succat, and for six years he tended the
herds of Milcho on the barren slopes of Slemish
Mountain in Antrim. Across the North Channel the boy could discern the cliffs of distant
Scotland. It was then that the memory of the
pirate raid would rise fresh within him.

He had been amusing himself at his father's
country villa in Wales, enjoying the harmless, idle
existence of a magistrate's son. His father, Cal-
purnius, was a Roman decurion and the family
was Christian. In those years the barbarian hordes
were pressing toward Rome, and soon the outlying provinces would be abandoned. Now,
however, life was easy and pleasant for Succat.

All of that changed when Niall of the Nine
Hostages, Ard-Ri (High King) of Ireland, swept
up from the sea with his warriors. The villa was
despoiled and Succat captured.

This boy—later to be known as Patrick, apostle to Ireland—was purchased by Milcho, a local
chieftain in northeast Ireland, and sent to herd
sheep and swine on Slemish. He climbed the
bare, basalt heights in crude leather sandals
laced with thongs. A sheepskin tunic fell to his
knees and his head was clean shaven as a mark
of servitude. His cruel master beat and cursed
him and fed him with the animals. Even the
elements tormented him as snow and hail and
rain and wind cut through his ragged garments.
Yet he survived, and he found on Slemish, in
suffering and solitude, the God undiscovered
in his former luxury. He learned to pray and he
learned that the fear of the Lord is the beginning of wisdom. In his loneliness he pledged
his life to the service of his Creator.

One night, his eyes weary from the watch and his nostrils full of the sea's luring scent, Patrick dozed upon the hillside, and a voice came to him in a dream, saying, "You have fasted well and soon will go to your own country."

Encouraged, the young man—for he was now twenty-two—persevered. He was rewarded a short time later when the same voice directed him to leave.

"Behold," it advised him, "your ship is ready."

Trusting the vision, Patrick set out on a two-hundred-mile journey down the alien coast, arriving exhausted but unmolested at a seaport where a large vessel awaited the tide. Its cargo was wolfhounds bred in Ireland for the Continent's noblemen. The crew was as savage as the hounds.

Patrick begged for passage, but the rough captain surveyed the ragged, penniless runaway and declared, "You shall by no means come with us!"

Turning his back on freedom, Patrick plodded inland. Was it to end like this? Had the vision mocked him?

One of the sailors called to him. "Come quickly," he ordered. "We'll take you on good faith. You can pay us when you're able."

And so Patrick embarked upon a new slavery as a Christian among pagans. After three days they landed somewhere in Britain but found only

desolation. During a month's journey, they saw
no other living person. Hunger stalked them,
threatening the enterprise and their very lives.

The merchant captain taunted Patrick. "Christian, do you not say that your God is great and
all-powerful? Why, then, can you not pray for
us since we are in danger of starving?"

"Nothing is impossible to God," replied Patrick. "He possesses everything in abundance."

At these words, a herd of swine crossed their
path and the men fell upon them and slaughtered
them. Refreshed, they led the dogs south. After
a few weeks, however, Patrick escaped and returned to his family.

Nearly twenty years pass, during which the
boy, Succat, becomes Patrick, the missionary.
How he spent each year is uncertain, but he
may have visited monasteries and hermitages in
Europe. Other scholars, basing their case on Patrick's Latin usage, contend that he studied ex-
clusively in Britain—specifically, Wales. His scattered seminary days were evidently happy ones,
and he became well versed in Scripture, administration, and the techniques of construction. The
simplicity, fervor and endurance which were the
legacy of Slemish were now augmented by the
virtues of wisdom and conviction.

During these long years, he dreamed continu-
ally of Ireland. In a vision he received letters from

an angelic courier, in one of which he read the words, "The Voice of the Irish." As he stared at the letter, he seemed to hear the cries of these pagan people beckoning him.

"We entreat thee, holy youth, to come and walk once more among us."

His mission seemed clear: Ireland was to be his apostolate. But between that resolve and its fulfillment lay many obstacles and disappointments. His family objected and his superiors questioned his ability in the face of certain danger. His best friend turned against him and denounced him as unworthy of the assignment because of a youthful sin which Patrick had once confided to him.

Christian missionaries were not unknown in Ireland. Current scholarship places Palladius in Ireland about the time of Patrick's escape. For perhaps a decade, this earlier apostle, armed with authorization from Rome, worked with moderate success within a limited southern section of the island. He left or was forced out of the country and died, perhaps in Scotland. It is likely that the companions of Palladius, whose work is virtually lost to history, continued the mission into Patrick's time.

Unlike that of Palladius, Patrick's mission seems to have been a British mission. Perhaps a synod of British bishops dispatched him in answer to his repeated requests for the assignment. If that were so, he would be about forty when he set sail for Ireland. His initial route in the missionary territory is uncertain, but legend gives us one course which possesses drama, if not accuracy.

Touching first at Wicklow, Patrick was driven out, as Palladius had been before him. He steered north along the coast, skirting Dublin and Royal Meath, bypassing the sandy bays and rocky headlands of Louth, past Dundalk Bay and the bulky hill of Slieve Donard, arriving, finally, at Strangford Lough. Through the foaming strait joining the lake to the sea, he piloted the small craft. Gliding past tiny islands and green woodland, he beached the boat in the shadow of the misty Mountains of Mourne and climbed toward a rude barn where he celebrated Mass.

Here Patrick was discovered by a shepherd of Dichu, a local chieftain, who raced to the scene with his warriors. Instead of finding raiders, he encountered Patrick and fell under his spell. He became the missionary's first convert and deeded him the land and barn for a church. This place is now called Saul—from Sabhall Padraic, the barn of Patrick.

Through the winter the small band shared the hospitality of Dichu, but hardly had the snow begun to melt in the hills before Patrick left for

Tara. It was there the High King lived, and Patrick wanted his official sanction.

This procession arrived at Tara on Easter Sunday, as has been related. Patrick, arrayed in white and carrying his staff as a crozier, led them into King Leary's court where it had been decreed no man should show him any honor. When Patrick marched between the rows of shields, however, many warriors could not refrain from bowing.

The Ard-Ri never accepted Christianity, but he gave Patrick permission to preach and baptize. Within King Leary's court many converts were made. This was the beginning of an incredible record of missionary activity. Patrick roamed Ireland, baptizing thousands; some accounts say, "hundreds of thousands." He erected hundreds of churches or places of worship, ordained more than 3000 priests, and, since every clan wanted its own bishop, he consecrated no less than 370 prelates. When one considers that he entered a strange land with few native allies, confronted with a highly organized pagan culture and burdened with increasing age, his success is all the more startling. And he accomplished all this without bloodshed.

He marched across the land with an efficient, self-sufficient entourage composed of priests, judges, a bodyguard, a psalmist, cooks, various

tradesmen and artisans, seminarians and other use-
ful retainers. They were capable of building a
church from the ground up. Usually the sites of
Patrick's principal churches reflected his knowledge of the political complexion of the land, for
he located them in the territories of strong kings
and princes.

Through Connaught he moved, baptizing
Ethna and Fedelma, daughters of the King.
One touching story has these two young girls
receiving the Holy Eucharist and then dying of
their desire to see Christ.

Then back to Meath and through Leinster
where the crowds from Dublin rushed out to
hear him preach. South next, to Munster, where,
at royal Cashel, sometime in the 480's, King
Aongus was received into the faith.

At the baptism of Aongus, Patrick, striking the
ground with his pointed staff, accidentally drove
it through the foot of the King. Uncomplaining,
Aongus suffered through the rite. When the apol-
ogetic saint asked why he had not called out,
Aongus replied, "I thought it was part of the
ceremony."

Not all of Patrick's attempts were successful.
Early in his missionary life he traveled to
Slemish to bring the Christian faith to his former
tormentor, Milcho. This pagan, fearing Patrick's
power and the shame of being converted by his

former slave, set fire to his home and died in the blaze. Like Christ over Jerusalem, tradition tells us, Patrick stood above the ashes and wept.

There were dangers in his mission—hunger, thirst, perils of land and sea voyages, weariness. Sometimes his brethren turned on him or his foes made attempts on his life. His brave charioteer once took a spear-thrust meant for Patrick. Mostly, though, Patrick's life consisted of prayer and work and then more prayer and more work.

Rarely was he free for contemplation. Once he spent the forty days of Lent upon Croagh Patrick, a symmetrical cone of white quartzite which rises above Clew Bay. Here he fasted alone and prayed. An angel came to confer with him. From this heavenly messenger, Patrick extracted, it is said, promises that the Irish would hold fast to the faith until the end of time; that a tidal wave would inundate the island seven years before the Last Judgement, thus sparing his people the frightful spectacle; that no enemy would ever hold Ireland by force or consent while Patrick was in heaven; and that every Irishman doing penance, even in the last hour, would not be doomed to hell on the last day.

On one point, it is said, the angel demurred. The saint requested that, on the Day of Doom, "I myself shall be judge of the men of Erin."

When the angel rendered the opinion that this promise could not be had from God, Patrick threatened to remain on the mountain until his wish was granted. After a hurried round-trip to heaven, the story goes, the angel returned and explained that, after a long discussion in which Patrick was praised for every virtue except his obstinacy, God had finally acceded to his request.

"All the men of Erin, living or dead," announced the angel, "shall be blessed and consecrated to God through thee."

To this day, Croagh Patrick remains a place of special pilgrimage among the many sites connected with the missionary saint.

Toward the end of his life Patrick established himself at Armagh, two miles from the legendary fortress of Emain Macha. His cathedral was of stone and much larger than the small basilicas which served him elsewhere. A school and a monastery followed, and other schools grew up around the site. Within two centuries it became one of the great universities of the civilized world.

Some of Patrick's personal writings have come down to us, and other canons, proverbs and poems are ascribed to his pen. In the famed "Epistle to Coroticus" we see a saint inflamed with righteous anger. This scorching letter was directed against a British prince who had raided

Ireland and carried off some of Patrick's converts as slaves.

"Is it a crime to be born in Ireland?" wrote Patrick. "Have we not the same God as you?"

He denounces the raiders as "rebels against Christ" and asks, "What manner of hope in God have you, or any who cooperate with you? God will judge!"

More famous, of course, is Saint Patrick's autobiographical work, the "Confession." Written to defend himself against some unfair criticism, it contains a digest of his early life and trials, the record of his mission in Ireland, a sampling of his prayers and philosophy. Throughout, his character stands forth, beginning with these humble opening lines:

"I, Patrick, a sinner, the most rustic and the least of all the faithful, and, in the estimation of many, deemed contemptible . . ."

and concluding:

"But I pray for those who believe and fear God, whosoever will have deigned to look upon this writing which Patrick, the sinner and unlearned no doubt, wrote in Ireland, that no one shall ever say it was my ignorance through which I have done God's will; but think, and let it be most firmly believed, that it was the gift of God. And this is my Confession before I die."

Death was not far away for Patrick. His last years were spent as his early years—building, baptizing, ordaining. The responsibility for the Irish mission demanded most of his energy. He must have traveled less, headquartering principally at Armagh. It was here he wished to die. God's plans, however, were different.

One of his chroniclers tells us that Patrick, having a premonition of death, was hastening back to Armagh from a tour through the province when an angel halted him and told him to return to Saul, where he had built his first church and made his first converts. Sadly but obediently, he turned back to the shores of Strangford Lough, and there he died on March 17th, 493.

Several communities contended for the honor of burial. Legend has it that the arguments were settled by placing the corpse, wrapped in its shroud, upon a cart drawn by two white oxen. The beasts were given their heads, and they wandered southwest a few miles, to Downpatrick. It is here Saint Patrick's remains are said to lie, along with—so tradition tells us—the bones of Brigid and Columcille. This hallowed spot, in the churchyard adjoining the Downpatrick Cathedral, is identified by a large granite boulder which is marked with a cross and simply inscribed: PATRIC.

Very little is certain regarding Patrick's mission, and scholars have speculated extensively. Chief among the areas of dispute are the troublesome dates. One has to ignore the legends of the snakes and the shamrocks to find the courageous visionary with a practical energy who exiled himself from his homeland to transform a whole people into a Christian nation. History verifies the presence of other missionaries in Ireland at a somewhat earlier date, but in the hearts of the Irish Patrick will always be first, just as they were first in his heart.

"May God never permit it to happen to me," he once prayed, "that I should lose His people which He purchased in the utmost parts of the world."

(453?-524?) ST. BRIGID

CHAPTER TWO

"God's word to speak for me . . ."

St. Patrick's missionary zeal accomplished wonders in Ireland, but the country remained disor-
ganized and beset by internal strife. Leinstermen
fought with the High King over his annual levy
of cattle, and they struggled with the southern
Ui Neill for disputed midland territory. The Ui
Neills battled among themselves for the throne
at Tara. It was an untidy situation and called for
a woman's touch. Leinster, which provided the

arena for most of the conflict, also supplied the peacemaker in the person of St. Brigid, the "Mary of the Gael."

Second only to Patrick among the saints of Ireland, Brigid was born at Faughart in the middle of the fifth century. Legend surrounds her from the moment of birth, when angels were observed hovering over her mother's cottage at the foot of the Cooley Mountains, their brilliance illuminating near-by Dundalk Bay. Her father was Dubthach (Duffy), a pagan chieftain descended from Conn of the Hundred Battles and her mother a Christian slave named Brocessa. Soon after Brigid's birth, her mother was sold out of Dubthach's household to a Druid in Connaught. As slave, she could expect no consideration because of motherhood.

Slavery in Ireland had most of the evils inherent in it elsewhere. Women in servitude were chattel to be bartered. For the free woman, however, Ireland was the most enlightened of European countries. Near-equality for women existed from earliest times, permitting educational and professional opportunities, legal equity and, on some occasions, acceptance as warriors. In marriage, although the husband remained head of the household, the wife retained any property she brought with her and shared in the goods the couple owned jointly. While the women tradi-

tionally gathered apart at religious or festive occasions, they received all of the respect and
courtesy associated with the Age of Chivalry—
except that this behavior was genuine, not artifi-
cial.

Although in bondage to Dubthach, Brigid enjoyed many family privileges and moved amid a
free society. Despite her differences with her father, his status as a nobleman enhanced her mission and he must have aided her financially.

Brigid's youth, however, was not happy—except as she made it so. Separated from her
mother, she was given over to the care of a
nurse. As soon as she was old enough, she assumed her role as servant and ministered to
Dubthach. When free of her chores, she sought
solitude and the companionship of the dark
forest and the animals which inhabited it. Many
tales are told of Brigid during this period, some
similar to stories about St. Francis. It is said
that she once tamed a wild boar, making him
part of her father's herd. Another story tells
of her intercession on behalf of a condemned
slave who had accidentally killed the king's
pet fox. Riding to plead the serf's cause, Brigid
chanced upon another fox, presented him to the
king and bade the animal perform. The amateur
beast conducted himself in the manner of the pro-

fessional acrobat, winning the king's favor and sparing the slave's life.

While no portraits of Brigid exist, we are told by the earliest chroniclers that she was a beautiful girl, quick-witted, pleasant and capable. Her accomplishments testify to her vigor which, together with a resolute spirit, made her a woman difficult to withstand. Fortunately, mercy and charity tempered her strength.

Most of the legends center about Brigid's charitable deeds and their miraculous circumstances. Frequently she would empty the family larder to satisfy a beggar's hunger, only to have it replenished by the Lord. She was forever giving her master's belongings to the poor. This trait proved an irritation to Dubthach, who attempted to sell Brigid to the King of Leinster. While waiting in the royal courtyard to learn her fate, Brigid was accosted by a leper seeking alms. Having no money to give him, she reached into her father's chariot, removed his jeweled sword, and gave it to the poor wretch. When Dubthach returned to present her to the court, he missed his sword and upbraided her furiously. Thrusting her before King Dunlang, the pagan chieftain complained of the loss, but the king merely questioned Brigid patiently, asking why she had disposed of the sword which he had once presented to her father.

"Do not wonder that I have bestowed upon the poor that which was in my possession," she answered. "If it were in my power, I should give to them all possessed by my father and by you, O King. For the Almighty will confer eternal rewards on those who, for His sake, give temporal riches."

Dunlang was a Christian and he understood this girl. Turning to Dubthach, he advised, "Leave her alone. I have not the means for purchasing her since she is more precious than silver or gold. She stands higher before God than we. Let her choose her way in life."

He then gave Dubthach a sword more valuable than the one he had lost, and the chieftain took Brigid home, where he released her from slavery.

As she grew older, Brigid requested permission to visit her mother in Connaught. Refused, she left anyway, walking the long miles to the mountain where Brocessa tended the Druid's cattle. For a short time she labored beside her mother in the fields and in the dairy, where her charitable nature nearly betrayed her once more. Beggars appearing at the dairy were given whatever produce was available. When the Druid learned of this, he and his wife conducted a surprise inventory. To their amazement, they found more butter and cheese and milk than normal. Sensing the presence of sanctity, the Druid tried to bestow the entire herd upon Brigid. She asked, instead, for her mother's freedom and Brocessa's thralldom was ended.

Returning to her father's house, Brigid learned that Dubthach had selected a suitor for her, a poet of excellent character and reputation. In ancient Ireland poets shared the highest rank in the kingdom and were respected for their wisdom and skill. It was considered an excellent match by Brigid's family and friends.

Calmly, resolutely, she refused the offer of marriage, while telling the poet she would pray for his success with some other maiden. She announced her intention of remaining a virgin consecrated to the service of God.

How or why Brigid arrived at her decision is unknown. Attempts have been made to link her with St. Patrick, but this poses historical problems. One legend has Brigid nodding during one of Patrick's sermons and dreaming allegorically of their joint Christian conquest of Ireland. If, however, the traditional date of Patrick's death is accepted (461 A.D.), Brigid would have been a child of eight at the time. If 493 A.D. is considered, the story becomes plausible.

With or without the inspiration of St. Patrick, Brigid made a decision to adopt the monastic life and she left home forever, accompanied by seven virgins who formed Ireland's first religious community of women. Prior to this, girls who took holy vows merely remained at home, living and working as quietly as possible. Brigid changed all of this, giving real meaning to the Irish sisterhood.

The eight women traveled southwest to Croghan Hill where Bishop Mel officiated at the profession of their vows and placed the nun's veil on each of their heads. Once again a "fiery pillar" is said to have hovered above Brigid's head, and an amusing commentary states that the startled prelate misread his prayers and consecrated her a bishop by mistake.

Croghan Hill became the site of her first religious house and one of a number ascribed to her. Prayer, fasting, work and contemplation filled the hours of the holy women, but Brigid did not subscribe to a cloistered existence. Instead she traveled across Ireland, usually by chariot.

As with every phase of the saint's biography, there are numerous "chariot" tales representing miraculous escapes, daring rides and widespread conversions. In fact, she attracted so many pagans by her excursions that she was provided with a priest-chaplain as charioteer, and he performed the myriad baptisms.

Many miracles are attributed to Brigid during

this period. She is said to have had great medical skill and the power to heal the deaf and blind and to exorcise demons. Some of the miraculous deeds have Biblical overtones—multiplying bread, changing water into ale—and there are prophecies and visions which recall the Old Testament.

New communities flourished in Offaly, West Meath, in Munster and Connaught. Most famous of all Brigidine monasteries was the one she founded at Kildare, the "Cell of the Oak," sometime between 484 and 488. Larger than most monastic settlements, Kildare attracted priests and poets, saints and scholars. Like other communities, it was self-sustaining, living off the bounty of the surrounding land (which Brigid had claimed by miraculously spreading her cloak over twelve square miles of lovely hillside). Eventually, Kildare became a sizeable town and Brigid requested Conlaeth, a saintly recluse, to serve as its bishop. Conlaeth accepted, building Kildare into an outstanding religious center and earning for himself the title of "Brigid's Brazier."

All of Ireland knew of Brigid's hospitality and every visitor was welcome within her walls. Young girls came to stay the night and share her wisdom. Bishops traversed mountain and plain to meet this remarkable holy woman. Once a retinue of weary prelates arrived to preach to the nuns

but asked for supper first, since they were ex-
ceedingly hungry.

Brigid, always brief in speech, replied, "We
are hungry, too, for the word you bring us.
Preach first and then you shall be fed."

Brigid never lost her penchant for charity. A
valuable chain given to her by the Queen of
Leinster was bestowed upon a passing mendicant,
and her sister companions were sometimes vexed
at her habit of donating their meals to the poor.
On one occasion, a wealthy scamp disguised himself as a beggar and successfully cadged food
from Brigid. Each time he repeated this trick, he
returned home to find the previous goods missing.

Generous herself, Brigid was impatient with
selfishness in others. One legend relates that she
met a man bearing salt on his back and asked him
for some for her community. After refusing her,
the traveler continued on his way, feeling the
load becoming increasingly heavy. Slitting the
sack, he discovered that the salt had turned to
stone. His apology and offer to share his bounty
converted the burden back to salt.

Another pleasant tale treats of Brigid's visit to
a fortress in Limerick. Desiring music while she
waited, she asked someone to play the harp which
hung upon the castle wall. No one was able to
play. Brigid instructed an untrained youth to try,
and he produced beautiful music at the first

touch of his fingers. Moreover, his descendants became famous as harpists throughout Ireland.

Just as the shamrock is associated with St. Patrick, so is the tiny cross made of rushes linked to Brigid. While explaining the Passion to a dying pagan, she wove a cross from the rushes strewn about his floor. They are still made in Ireland today and placed in the rafters of cottages on St. Brigid's day (February 1) to ward off harm.

Ancient stories also give St. Brigid considerable political influence. She freed slaves of the nobility, instructed their offspring, and once prevented bloodshed between two princely brothers, Conall and Cairbre, by rendering their approaching armies invisible to one another.

Despite these sojourns into higher society, Brigid remains the saint of the common man. She dignified labor and sympathized with the working man. She was skilled as a cook and herdsman. Never sparing of her own energies, she was no Pharisee. Once she rebuked her nuns for exacting more penance of themselves than the Lenten fast required.

As death neared, St. Brigid was often alone, sunk in prayer and contemplation. St. Ninnid, a priest whom she first met as a young boy, was at her side to administer the Last Sacraments. It was in Kildare that she died, but her bones sup-

posedly now rest with those of Patrick and
Columcille at Downpatrick.

While her quick spirit was stilled, her name
lives on in a hundred places. Churches in Ireland,
England, Scotland, France and Germany established devotions in her memory. Two Bride
Rivers grace Ireland, and names like Kilbride and
Templebreedy bear her impression. Thousands of
girls adopt her name annually, and "Biddy" was
once a synonym for young colleens. Places associated with Brigid have become shrines and at-
tract vast throngs of pilgrims.

Most of all, she lives on in the character she
imparted to Irish Christianity, the humanizing,
humble values of compassion, charity and courage. Her virtue earned her the reputation of never
being denied by God. Perhaps this is because she
sought so little. A quaint poem attributed to her
closes with these lines:

> "I should like to be a rent-payer to the Lord;
> That should I suffer misfortune,
> He would bestow upon me a good blessing."

(484-577) St. Brendan

CHAPTER THREE

"God's strength to pilot me . . ."

Like Brigid, St. Brendan the Navigator was a man immersed in legend. The tales of his voyages, though lacking in historical evidence, formed one of the sources of Dante's *Divine Comedy* and inspired seafarers down to the time of Columbus. His name has been linked with the discovery of America and the mysterious appearance of Christianity among the Aztecs.

Yet Brendan was not a legend but a man—a

courageous, determined, zealous man. He represents the advent of the wandering Irish saints who were to sweep across the Continent, preaching, teaching and building. At the time of his birth, Christianity was firmly established in Ireland and internal conflict had subsided. The Roman Empire of the West was finished, and Theodoric, King of the Ostrogoths, reigned in Ravenna. In England, Britons retreated before Saxons, while both feared the raids of Irish pirates. It was a period of change and crisis, the beginning of the Middle Ages.

Brendan's parents, Finnlugh and Cara, were Christians and related by blood to the famed Niall of the Nine Hostages. They lived near Tralee in County Kerry where the tide probed inland beneath the slopes of hulking mountains. Brendan was one of five children—four boys and a girl. His birth was accompanied by glorious signs and wonders, marking him as one destined for great things.

Surrounded by the roaring surf, daring fishermen, and the beckoning offshore islands, the saint's early love for the sea is understandable. His first journey, however, was a land journey and occurred when he was scarcely a year old.

Bishop Erc, ruling prelate of the district, came to the crib of the newborn child like one of the

Magi, claiming Brendan as a foster son. In keeping with this assumed responsibility, the bishop sent his ward to a convent school for boys in Killeady, Limerick, to begin his education. The school was administered by St. Ita, called "The Brigid of Munster," and under her tutelage Brendan spent five formative years. He was six when he returned to Kerry and Bishop Erc.

The next fourteen years he spent as a student in a rude monastery on the seacoast, living in a cramped stone bee-hive cell, subsisting on a vegetarian diet with the first food taken at 3 P.M., and enduring the elements with patience and fortitude. Discipline was strict, both in the fields and in the classrooms, but Brendan had the frequent companionship of his sister, Briga, who submitted herself to the same monastic existence.

At the monastery Brendan learned Latin and perhaps Greek and Hebrew. History and mathematics must have been among his studies and since Erc, converted from Druidism by Patrick, knew the science of astronomy, he undoubtedly shared this knowledge with his students. The basis of Brendan's skill in navigation may be traced to the discussions he had with his bishop as both surveyed the Atlantic from Kerry's cliffs or as they rode the waves in a scallop-shell boat. During his waking hours Brendan studied, fished or farmed. At night he retired, weary and hun-

gry, to his wooden cot. He learned to accept
hardship. And he learned to dream.

Before completing the studies which would
lead him to the priesthood, Brendan, now twenty,
decided to travel across Ireland. Being poor, he
could afford no chariot, so he walked the narrow,
dusty roads in his worn sandals, supported by a
staff and clad in a thin tunic. Sometimes he had
companions; often he journeyed alone. After a
time he made his way north to the theological
school at Cluainfois. En route, he made his first
convert, Colman MacLenin, famed heathen war-
rior who was to become St. Colman.

The days at Cluainfois were followed by an
extended stay with relatives in Mayo. It was here,
at Magh Enna, that he formulated the monastic
rule which was to govern his life and the lives of
his future disciples.

At thirty years of age he came home and was
ordained by the dying Bishop Erc. Brendan's reputation for holiness—including a report that he
had raised a young man from the dead in Mayo
—attracted religious recruits to his side. Some
were fishermen; others were farmers, soldiers,
students. At Ardfert, the first of many monasteries founded by Brendan, this mixed community began to live by his order.

Other religious settlements followed—at Barrow, Rathoo, Kilfenora, and Brandon Hill.

Often the founder himself labored in the construction. Yet his mind was full of the sea and its challenge. The progress of his Irish activities caused him to look abroad for other souls to redeem.

Living by the ocean all of his life, Brendan had many opportunities to hear fables of distant lands, strange perils and mysterious beauty. Chief among the sailors' tales was the story of Tir-na-n-Og, the "Land of Youth," an earthly paradise lying to the west of Ireland beyond the setting sun. Every seventh year people claimed to see its shadowy form in the skies above Erin. Brendan found the call too insistent to ignore. Gathering his companions about him, he sought their judgement. They voted to set sail.

Forty days of prayer and fasting were followed by weeks of labor. With the help of his comrades, Brendan fashioned an oversized curragh—a ship having ribs of willow laced with wicker and cased in oak-tanned hides. A triangular sail was carried and a full set of spoon-shaped oars. Water-skins, dried fish, grain, roots and edible sea-moss were stored in the larder to feed the crew of fourteen. Some of the seamen were priests, and all were skilled sailors or artisans.

In autumn they prepared to depart, blessing both the ship and the Kerry harbor in the name

of the Holy Trinity. Three latecomers were
added to the crew when they threatened to
starve themselves unless taken aboard. Two turned
out to have evil intentions and met violent deaths
at sea, one being swept overboard and the other
being engulfed by molten lava near Iceland.

Where Brendan sailed on any of his many voyages is uncertain. The legends speak of mermaids,
and monster fish, and black dwarfs. They record
the mythical Isle of Fleas and Isle of Mice and
the Isle of Perpetual Day. Satan hurls hot iron
at Brendan's ship and a huge cat threatens to
swamp it. Many of the details, however, are
credible.

As the ship departed from Ireland, Brendan set
no course but trusted in Divine Providence to
guide its meanderings to the promised isle. For
two weeks they were driven north. Then the sea
calmed, leaving them stranded for a similar period. At length they landed in the Hebrides, refreshed themselves, and continued to the Faroe
Islands where they slaughtered sheep for food.

Easter found them abreast of a small island
where they decided to conduct a service. When
the rite was concluded, one of the crew attempted to light a fire. The "island" heaved,
sending the sailors scurrying for the curragh.
They then learned they had boarded a whale!

An erratic wind whirled them southeast toward the Shetlands. The ship was straining and the crew edgy, but Brendan maintained discipline. Food ran low, restricting the voyagers to a single meal every second or third day.

Things changed when they debarked on the main island of the Shetlands. Here they met a community of Irish monks who had lived on the island for eighty years. Brendan and his companions were feasted, bathed and rested. In return, they told the news from Ireland. When it came time to depart, the hermit brethren wept.

More haphazard navigation ensued in the North Atlantic, not due to Brendan's lack of skill but to his excess of faith. When nautical problems did arise, he reacted well and kept the ship secure. One problem, however, he could not relieve. Food and water petered out and he was forced to steer for the nearest land. Once ashore, his parched crew disobeyed his command and drank from a fetid stream. The resulting illness idled the ship as Brendan nursed them back to health.

Afloat once again, they were buffeted by heavy seas and chilling gales. For three months, while they huddled for comfort on the small craft, the storms tossed and tormented them. Brendan called out to the turbulent ocean, "O mighty sea, if you must, take me alone to drown. Spare these others—my people!"

The storm continued, forcing them back to Shetland where they spent the Christmas season. When the dark skies lifted and the waters composed themselves, Brendan sailed north again, skirting lonely Rockall Island and landing at the Vestmannaejar (Irishman's) Islands, south of Iceland, where the steaming lava claimed the life of a troublesome crew member. After a brief stay on Iceland, where they encountered another colony of Irish monks, the little curragh drifted south.

Once again they dropped anchor in the Faroes, and on a craggy peninsula Brendan met Paul, reputedly the first hermit. One story has Paul convincing Brendan that he should return to Ireland. Another legend relates that Brendan was unable to land on this island but that a note was lowered from the cliffs, reading, "This is not your promised country. You shall reach it one day, but, for now, go home to your family."

Whatever the reason, Brendan elected to return to Erin. He had not sighted the Isle of Youth, so he considered the voyage a sterile venture. By candlelight he glided into Brandon Bay. He had been absent for five years and his friends and disciples mourned him as dead. With them this Christian Ulysses spent several happy weeks, but his soul was restless and his quest unfulfilled. The vision of the Happy Isle still lingered.

Bewildered by his initial failure, Brendan visited St. Ita, his foster mother, and sought her counsel. She offered the practical suggestion that he cooperate more fully with God in navigation and that he equip a larger ship with a serviceable rudder.

Taking her advice, Brendan supervised the construction of a massive oak vessel, caulked with tar, and fitted with an iron anchor. It boasted a single woven sail, a solid deck above the storage compartment—and a rudder. Grain and plants were carried, plus live pigs and dried fish and sea-holly for protection against scurvy. Water-skins were supplemented by wooden casks, and there were spare parts for the ship—iron, rope, pegs, sailcloth and other items. Three trained ravens were taken aboard to signal the proximity of land.

The volunteer crew of sixty included priests, lay monks, sailors and technicians. Crosan, the king's jester, signed on, as did St. Malo and Moenniu, Brendan's successor at Clonfert. In late March, 551, a great crowd swarmed to the sea-shore to bid them farewell.

By day, they steered by the sun; at night, the North Star was their beacon. West from the Aran Islands they scudded, piercing fog and skirting icebergs until they sighted New-foundland. Unable to beach the ship, they anchored offshore and observed walrus, gulls, loons and herons.

Crosan became ill and received the Last Sacraments. Although reputed to be a great sinner in the past, he was a favorite among the sailors.

"What good have I done to deserve this death?" he whispered, as he expired in Brendan's arms. His sea burial took place in a sheltered cove.

The ship's smith also died and was dropped into the ocean as the curragh turned south by east. Except for a waterspout which terrified the crew momentarily, the cruise was smooth and uneventful until they reached the Bahama Islands. Here the natives appeared warlike, and Brendan, wishing to avoid bloodshed, made no attempt to land.

While sitting offshore, they made repairs and tried to salvage a fouled anchor. Eventually they had to cut the anchor loose and were faced with the problem of forging a new one. With the smith dead, the task fell to a priest who used a combination of prayer and perspiration to complete the job.

On the largest of the Bahama islands, it is said, they put ashore and met a lonely Irish monk. Before they could converse, they were interrupted by a battle between a giant cat and a shark. The struggle threatened to swamp the curragh. The monk explained that the sea-cat had once been a small kitten when he and eleven companions adopted and fed it. The kitten grew to giant size, however, killing the other monks. He, alone, remained. With these words, he collapsed and died, receiving the Last Rites from Brendan.

The wind bore them westward, past blue lagoons and beds of coral, as the odor of spice and magnolia and lotus and hibiscus filled the air. As they spied the verdant coast of Florida, singing birds circled their ship, welcoming them. Believing they had reached the "Land of Promise," the mariners chanted a grateful "Te Deum" and stepped ashore on the white sand. Brendan dubbed the land "Hy Brasil," and so it appears on ancient charts.

Once again they met an old Irish monk, a resident of Florida for thirty years. Convinced they were on an island, Brendan and his companions struck out for the western shore, trekking through swamps and rain forests, meeting alligators and hummingbirds and watchful Indians. At length, legends tell us, they came to a great, impassable river—the Mississippi, perhaps—and had to turn back to their ship. With the hermit monk, Festivus, they spent several weeks, and then Brendan announced they would sail for home. Perhaps it was homesickness again. Perhaps it was Brendan's realization that there was still

much work to be done in Ireland and that the
Land of Promise might be a romantic distraction.
Leaving Festivus with a supply of food, they
took aboard some gold, fruit and flowers and
steered for the Aran Islands. The round trip had
consumed two years.

While proof of this voyage is lacking and
while there are many obvious fantasies included,
it cannot be denied that the trip was possible. The
Vikings made similar journeys, and Pacific Is-
landers drifted thousands of miles in strange
waters. According to Shawnee Indian traditions,
an Irish-speaking tribe existed in Florida, and
Columbus was reputedly interested enough to
read the accounts of Brendan's voyages and to
include some Irish seamen on his roster. When
Cortez invaded Mexico in 1519, he came across
the legend of Quetzalcoatl—"The Precious"—a
white-bearded missionary who had come from a
holy isle to the northeast, propelled by wings—
or sails. Could these be traces of Brendan's influence? The riddle has no answer. Recent discov-
eries have merely enhanced the possibilities—and
deepened the mystery.

When Brendan returned to Aran, amid great
rejoicing, he found his countrymen traveling for
miles to sit at his feet and hear him recount his
adventures. They would pass these tales along to

their children and grandchildren. Then the Gaelic scribes would enter and preserve them in colorful manuscripts.

For a time Brendan retired to an island in the Shannon River where he erected a monastery and spent the long days in prayer and fasting. This solitary life was not his destiny, however, for he was soon consecrated a bishop and sent throughout Ireland, building churches, teaching religion and navigation, mediating in court cases.

At Anaghdown in Galway, Brendan constructed a convent for his faithful sister, Briga, and her community of religious. He also taught at Clonard before proceeding to the foundation of his great monastic university at Clonfert. Thousands of students came from all over Europe to attend this institution on the banks of the Shannon.

It is said that Brendan put to sea again during this period. One story speaks of this voyage as penance for a rash act he committed. Another has him obeying a command of St. Ita to spread the Gospel. Scotland and Wales were on his itinerary, and here he visited Gildas the Wise and King Arthur of Cornwall. With Arthur he is reputed to have defended his former shipmate, St. Malo, against attack in Brittany.

Where his wandering curragh next docked is

lost even to legend. Some say he visited Palestine,
and Greece, and Egypt and the Canary Islands.
Whatever his ports of call, Brendan was absent
ten years from his native Ireland, returning in his
ninetieth year to a people who admired and re-
vered him. Brendan never wrote his own account
of his travels. Humility may have stopped his pen,
or perhaps the feeling that his voyages had been
foolish and worthless.

Weary and spent, he made his way to Anaghdown and Briga. Here his final illness struck him.
Finishing his Sunday Mass, he turned to his
friends and begged them to pray for his happy
death. His sister asked what he had to fear.

"I fear going alone," he replied, "for the way
is dark. I fear the unknown, the presence of the
king, the sentence of the judge."

At the chapel door he collapsed and died. According to his wishes his body was conveyed to
Clonfert for burial. All Ireland mourned him,
great and small. St. Columba led his community
in a sorrowful requiem. Far from the sea, Brendan's spirit came at last to rest.

All that remains at Clonfert are the ruins of the
cathedral. But Brendan is everywhere. His name
appears in Galway and Mayo, in Kerry and
Aran. His churches are in Scotland and Wales, in
the outer Hebrides and across the Continent. His
name is invoked by modern seafarers:

"St. Brendan, help us to remember that we have only one true port—Heaven. Help us never to suffer shipwreck on our journey thither, nor to put our souls in danger of sin which is the only true death. Pray for our land and our homes and make us know and love our faith more and more."

(521-597) st. columcille

CHAPTER FOUR

"God's eye to look before me . . ."

Among native Irish saints, Columcille holds the highest place. His body is said to lie 'at Downpatrick, beside those of Patrick and Brigid with whom he shares international veneration. His memory is enshrined not only in Ireland, but in England, Scotland and the Hebrides. Much of his charm lay in his essentially Celtic character—devout, fiery, energetic, romantic and able.

Columcille's kinsmen were the Ui Neill kings

of Tyrone and Tyrconnell. His father, Feid-limid, was a northern prince and his mother, Ethna, a descendant of Cathair Mor, founder of the royal line of Leinster. Born to nobility, Columcille might have been a great chieftain had he not chosen Christ as his commander.

The future saint was born at Gartan, County Donegal, on a grey December day in 521. His home jutted from a hillside overlooking Gartan Lough and facing the Glendowan Mountains to the west. He was baptized Crimthain, but his youthful frequenting of a neighboring chapel earned him the more familiar name of Columcille, meaning "dove of the church."

According to the ancient custom, the priest who christened him sent the boy to the Clan O'Freel for fosterage. Here, among the dark mountain passes, he performed his earliest miracles, and tales of them persist over turf fires in the Sperrin Mountains and the Valley of the Roe.

The boy's first formal schooling occurred at Moville, County Down, where St. Finnian was his mentor. Later he learned the art of poetry from Gemman, the Bard of Leinster. Finnian of Clonard helped him complete his education. At this monastic house he was instructed to erect his hut nearest the church, for he was held in great favor by Finnian. Making friends easily, Columcille soon became the acknowledged leader of a dozen seminarians, many of them becoming his lifelong companions.

With one of these students, his cousin, Bauheen, he traveled through the northern provinces, seeking a bishop to ordain them. Filled with the enthusiasm of youth, they had determined that this prelate must be an extraordinary man. They found such a man in Bishop Etchen whom they discovered ploughing his own field. Before agreeing to confer Holy Orders, the bishop finished his task. Such resolve they found worthy of imitation.

Following his ordination, Columcille spent some time at Glasnevin, near Dublin, where he was subject to St. Mobhi. His studies were interrupted in 544 when the Yellow Plague swept across the Continent, dispersing the students and sending Columcille north once more.

At Derry he founded his first monastery upon an oak-studded hill surmounting an arc of the River Foyle. Of all the sites inhabited by this migrant saint, Derry was his first and truest love. It is recorded that he feared less the demons of Hell than the sound of an axe in Derry wood. When he sailed away from Ireland, it was Derry he recalled in a plaintive ode attributed to him:

> "For her quietness, for Derry I care,
>   For the peace that is on her I love her.
>   White angels go crowding by there
>   From one end to another.

My Derry, my little oak grove,
My dwelling, my mansion of prayer.
O God in the heavens above
Bring woe to him who plunders there."

Derry was but one of thirty-six monasteries founded by Columcille. Swords, Screen, Drumcolum, Drumcliff, Drumhome and Kilglass were others. Durrow and Kells each produced invaluable manuscripts which may have been fashioned in Columcille's time. While building the monastic houses, Columcille may have spent some time in France, perhaps purchasing a rare Bible at Tours. Perhaps, too, he had a hand in the conversion of Tory Island off the coast of Donegal.

The inevitable legends crept into his biography. It is said that as a youth he conversed with angels and that one of them, Axel, became his permanent guardian. Columcille is credited with healing the sick, raising the dead, changing water into wine, calming stormy waters, subduing wild beasts and driving out unclean spirits. On one occasion he caused a stone to float, and on another he drew water from a rock.

While resting one day from his labor, he bit into some fruit and found it acrid. Inquiring as to the source, he was led to a wizened tree in the monastic orchard. He blessed the tree, and from that day forth it bore the sweetest fruit in the grove.

His gift of prophecy is cited in a hundred cases. He foretold sudden visits, deaths of kings and outcomes of battles. He knew who would rule and who would found churches. He could see into the hearts of men, divining their intentions, detecting their charity or malice.

When he was forty-two, he left Ireland, an exile. The circumstances surrounding his departure are vague. No doubt it was a common missionary excursion, but legend links his banishment to a rash and sanguine act.

During a visit to his old teacher, Finnian of Moville, Columcille was supposedly shown a newly acquired manuscript containing the four Gospels. He desired to have a copy of this for his monasteries in the west, so he crept into the library each evening and, by the light of a single candle, swiftly traced the exquisite letters onto a fresh parchment. Before Finnian discovered his intent, Columcille had transcribed the entire volume. The old monk was furious and demanded Columcille's duplicate. His guest refused and the matter was referred to Dermott, the High King, for arbitration. After pondering the evidence, the king delivered his famous verdict.

"To each cow her calf," he said, "and to each book its copy."

Columcille smoldered under the judgement and

resented the king who pronounced it. Soon he had additional cause to dislike Dermott.

Prince Curnan, a relative of Columcille, accidentally killed a contestant in the athletic games at Tara. Hunted as a murderer, he took sanctuary with Columcille, but Dermott's troops pursued him, violated the sacred refuge, and carried Curnan away to his death.

Inflamed by these grievances, Columcille encouraged the Ui Neills to war against Dermott. At Cuildremne in Sligo, the two forces met, and Columcille's kinsmen won a bloody victory in which three thousand warriors lost their lives.

Defeated, but still king, Dermott convoked a synod at Tailte. Summoned before this ecclesiastical body, Columcille heard the sentence of excommunication passed upon him for his part in the conflict. St. Brendan of Birr, however, braved the council's wrath by stepping to Columcille and kissing him. The act caused the synod to reconsider and the ban was lifted.

Columcille, now sick with guilt, fled to Devenish Island in Lough Erne and confessed his sin to St. Molaise. A severe penance was imposed.

"You will leave your land and your kindred— forever. You shall behold them no more but shall travel in foreign lands, winning as many souls for Christ as were slain at Cuildremne."

Sadly, Columcille gathered a dozen compan-

ions and sailed northeast in a bobbing curragh.
From the stern of his ship, he watched his homeland disappear.

> "There is a grey eye
>   That will look back upon Erin:
>   It shall never see again
>   The men and women of Erin.
>
> I strain my glance across the sea
>   From the firm oak planks;
>   Many are the tears of my soft grey eye
>   As I look back upon Erin."

Toward Scotland Columcille drifted, to a land
where his people, the Celts, had migrated in years
past. He would bring the Gospel to them and to
their enemies, the fierce Picts. With courage and
confidence, he beached his boat on the tiny island
of Iona at the southwestern tip of Mull in Scotland's western waters. From here, on a clear day,
he could see Ireland rising from the mist two
dozen leagues away.

On this colorful isle—a blend of green grasses,
jagged rock and pale stretches of sand—Columcille began his Scottish mission. His monastery
faced Mull and the mainland across a narrow
strait of clear blue water with seaweed shifting
in its depths. From Ireland came more priests to
join Columcille in his Christian conquest.

From Iona the saint moved inland, sailing up

perilous lakes to remote villages or preaching in the wild glens with the sound of wind in the birches, the cry of a curlew and the sweet scent of heather. The Scottish Druids opposed him, but his strength and faith overcame them.

At Inverness the pagan priests of King Brude locked the castle gates against Columcille. The missionary made the Sign of the Cross before the massive portal and it flew open, the bolts being drawn back as if by a powerful hand. Brude and his subjects were all converted.

Columcille sailed through the Hebrides, the Orkney and the Shetland Islands. Some accounts have him cruising to the Faroe Islands and Iceland. His missionary brethren were dispatched to Northumbria, to the Isle of Man, and to southern Britain.

When not at sea, Columcille played host to many visitors. Cronan of Munster came and Comgall of Bangor and the two intrepid voyagers, Brendan and Cormac. Sometimes a stranger would call across the narrow strait and the saint would row across to fetch him. Even in an age of hospitality, his friendly welcome was remarkable. One story illustrates this quality.

Once Columcille prophesied to a brother monk: "In three days, go early in the morning to the western shore of this island. At the ninth hour, a crane, weary and driven before the wind,

will descend to our beach. Lift it tenderly and
carry it to some neighboring cottage where, for
three days, it shall be nursed to health. Then will
it wing its way back to Ireland. I am anxious about this bird because it comes from my
home in Donegal."

The incident occurred as the saint predicted,
causing his community to marvel at his foresight
and his charity.

Columcille's fame spread. He became spiritual
counselor to King Conall, ruler of the Irish
Kingdom in Scotland. At the king's death, the
people looked to Columcille to crown his successor. The saint had decided to select Iogenan,
Conall's eldest son, but on three successive nights
an angel appeared to him and revealed a glass
tablet on which was written the command that
Aedhan, the youngest, should be king. Each time
Columcille refused to heed the message until, on
the third night, the angel scourged him and he
submitted. Aedhan's coronation was the first such
Christian ceremony recorded in Britain.

Soon after, Columcille had visitors from Ireland. They were poets who asked him to return
with them to testify in their behalf at the Council
of Drimceatt (574 A.D.). The new High King
had called this council to decide the fate of the
bardic brotherhood.

Poets in Ireland were a privileged profession,

having claim to the highest place at table and the choicest food. At any castle where they chanced to stop, they were to be housed in the finest suite of rooms for as long as they desired to stay. If these conditions were not fulfilled, the bards would compose a satire against the lord of the castle, bringing disgrace upon him and his household. Under these circumstances, it is small wonder that the ranks of the poets expanded and that the members became more overbearing and obnoxious. The nobles demanded that their craft be abolished. When one of them had the temerity to request the High King's brooch as a gift, the council was called to consider this supression.

Columcille realized the injustices committed by the poets, but he was one with them in talent and hated to see them dissolved. Yet he was under obligation not to set eyes upon home or friends. Neatly resolving this issue, the saint returned to Erin, his cowl drawn down about his face. Thus blinded, he was led to Drimceatt, and here he delivered an eloquent plea to save the poets.

"What remains of Cormac mac Art?" he asked the assembly. "Nothing but an empty skull dug from the side of a hill. Were it not for the poets to sing of his glories, his memory

would have died with his person. Who will sing
of future kings if the poets be banished?"

A courtier rebuked him. "We have other
things to think of, Columcille, besides fables."

Columcille retorted, "If the poets' verse be
fable, then all of your knowledge is fable. All
your rights and states and power and this drift-
ing world is fable."

Thus did Columcille, his face dark beneath his
hood but his sweet voice ringing clear, plead for
the poets. His oratory saved them, although he
agreed to restrictions placed upon their growth
and upon their authority. While at Drimceatt,
he also advised the High King to permit Aedhan to rule independently in Scotland in return
for an annual tribute.

After visiting a few of the churches he had
founded, Columcille returned to exile in Iona.
Perhaps he visited Ireland once again before his
death, but nothing is known of this voyage. Iona
was both his prison and his pride.

Each night he slept upon a flagstone with a
rock for a pillow. Each day he spent in prayer,
in labor, in reading and in writing. Three hundred books have been attributed to him. He had
lived a full life and he was in his seventy-sixth
year.

One Sabbath he called Diarmud, his attendant,
to him and confided that this would be his last

day upon earth. He inspected his swollen granaries and teeming fields and he was satisfied. That evening he summoned his monks and gave them his final counsel:

> "Be at peace with one another and cherish sincere charity. If you thus follow the example of the holy fathers, God, the comforter of the good, will assist you and I will intercede for you. He will not only minister to your needs in this life but will bestow upon you the eternal rewards that are prepared for those who obey His commandments."

To guard against idleness, even in his final hours, he sat at his desk to continue copying a manuscript. He came to the verse of the twenty-third Psalm which reads: "They that seek the Lord shall not be deprived of any good."

Here he ceased writing, remarking, "Let Baithen write the words which follow."

He arranged for Baithen, his successor, to take up his pen at the passage: "Come, children, hearken to me, I will teach you the fear of the Lord."

Early in the morning, while it was yet dark, Columcille made his way to the chapel. The watchful monks saw a light illumine the church, then falter and die. Groping their way in the blackness, they discovered their founder prostrate before the altar. Slowly lifting his hand, Columcille blessed his brothers. Then he quietly died.

For three days and three nights, Columcille
was waked and his body afterward interred in
the small cemetery of Iona. Here it rested, legend
tells us, until Viking raiders, seeking plunder, set
the coffin adrift in the Atlantic. It floated straight-
way to Downpatrick to join Patrick and Brigid
in death. A less romantic version tells us that
John de Courcy, a twelfth-century nobleman,
collected the bones of Columcille and transferred them to the site of the new cathedral at
Downpatrick.

Wherever his body rests, Columcille's spirit is
still abroad. His name graces churches in Spain
and the New World and his protection is invoked
by fishermen in the Hebrides. His successors
brought Christianity to most of Britain, and gen-
erations of poets have become his debtors. Until
recent times, Irish immigrants would spend the
eve of their departure near the rock marking his
birthplace in Donegal. To the exile they directed
their prayer, knowing he would understand.

(540? - 615) St. Columban

CHAPTER FIVE

"God's way to lie before me . . ."

Like St. Columcille, St. Columban was destined to die on alien soil. His exile, however, was self-imposed and it brought him fame as the first of the great Irish missionaries to the Continent.

This labor for Christ was foretold in a dream of Columban's mother. She saw a light shining from her own breast, a phenomenon her neighbors interpreted as a sign that her unborn child should bring faith to many. Before he could fulfill this prophecy, Columban had to bring grief to this woman who gave him life.

His birthplace was Leinster, perhaps the Carlow-Kildare region bounded by the Rivers Slaney and Barrow. During his formative years he remained at home where a tutor educated him. In this manner he reached his late teens, a serious young man, handsome and charming. Women were attracted to him, but their attentions caused him great concern. Bewildered, he sought counsel from a woman hermit living near by.

"Do you think you can go freely in the company of women?" she asked. "Do you not remember that Adam fell through the blandishments of Eve, that Samson was seduced by Delilah, that David fell from grace through the loveliness of Bethsabee and that Solomon was deceived by the love of women? Go, child, and turn away from the ruin into which many have fallen."

Columban resolved to quit the world and its temptations and adopt the celibate life of the priesthood. His mother begged him to remain with her and even attempted to bar his exit with her prostrate body. Sadly, the young man stepped over her, saying, "I will see you no more in this life, Mother, but wherever the path of holiness leads, there will I follow."

This path took him first to a scholarly reli-

gious named Sinell, a disciple of Finnian of Clonard. At Sinell's community at Cleenish on Lough
Erne, Columban spent five years studying Latin,
Sacred Scripture and Church History. His vocation was stronger than ever as he left for Bangor to become a monk.

Bangor, located on the sandy shores of
Lough Erne, was one of the most famous houses
of study in ancient Ireland. Students from many
lands gathered there under the strict but tem-
perate rule of St. Comgall. Here Columban
studied, prayed, fasted, and did penance. The
fare was simple and scant and the accommoda-
tions limited to cramped wattle huts ringing
the monastic church. For more than a decade
this was Columban's world. In it he must have
been happy and he must have excelled. So it
was with deep regret that Abbot Comgall heard
his most promising monk ask permission to
leave. After debating the matter, he agreed to
Columban's request.

If we accept the year 540 as Columban's
birthdate, he was in his thirty-fifth year when
he began his journey with twelve companions.
Among these was St. Gall, who would attend
Columban constantly, and young Domoal, who
would be his minister. Perhaps they voyaged
first to Britain. Some accounts have them stop-
ping in Cornwall. If so, it was a brief sojourn

and they soon crossed the Channel, landing in France. They had neither plan nor program but trusted in God to guide their steps.

Gaul, as France was known at that time, was torn by civil conflicts which raged for years among the descendants of Clovis, the Germanic founder of the Frankish kingdom. Into this land the thirteen missionaries ventured, moving eastward, preaching, teaching and converting. Gall may have acted as interpreter during these early days, or the group may have utilized Latin-German vocabularies which were available in script form. In this manner they came to the court of Sigibert, King of Austrasia, in 574, and revealed the Gospel to him.

King Sigibert was impressed with the zeal and with the spiritual message imparted by Columban. He begged the Irishmen to remain in his kingdom and offered them a remote tract of land to serve the pioneer community.

At Annegray, in the Vosges Mountains, Columban found the retreat he sought. The ruins of a Roman fort were the only civilized touch in this wild and desolate region. While laboring to construct the rude huts and refectory, Columban and his companions existed on herbs, roots and tree bark. One missionary collapsed. His brother monks then abstained from all food for three days and spent their time in prayer for his recovery.

On the third day, they had a visitor—a neighbor leading a packhorse laden with bread, vegetables and other provisions. His heart had led him to share his worldly goods with these men who suffered for Christ. In return for his generosity, the community prayed for their benefactor's sick wife and she was cured at that moment.

Other neighbors reacted in a similar fashion, delivering food as a response to a vision or merely because they realized the monks had no means of sustaining themselves. At length the buildings were complete, the first harvest bore fruit, and the near-by streams provided fish for the monastery table. Visitors were many and some remained to share the monastic life with Columban.

The preaching and ploughing went on, side by side. The community prospered in its simple way. Columban found even this isolated settlement a bit too active for contemplation, so he sought a solitary cell in the surrounding woods.

Jonas, the saint's biographer, tells us that Columban approached a likely cave but found the original tenant—a bear—unwilling to vacate. A few words from the Irish monk and the bear moved on. This skill with bears finds its way into a number of tales about Columban. Another story deals with a bear who was stealing fruit from a monastic orchard. Columban remonstrated with the beast and then compromised, giving the bear half of the grove. The obedient animal never crossed the forbidden boundary.

Another miracle is credited to Columban as he resided in the cave. Domoal, youngest of the missionaries, had the chore of carting water up the hill to Columban, a task which brought forth a complaint from Domoal. Columban recommended that he tap an adjacent rock and the deed resulted in a flow of fresh water which continues to this day.

Annegray's growth set Columban thinking of expansion. At Luxeuil, and later at Fontaines, he built new monasteries, at first presiding over all three. Separate abbots were installed eventually.

Luxeuil became famous and attracted many applicants, particularly from among the Burgundians. The monks lived under a strict rule which has often been criticized but which reflects Columban's austerity and vigor and his intense nature. Yet it reveals, too, that he knew men and that he knew monks. The various types of penance, including blows with a knout and enforced silence, were imposed for minor infractions, but Columban seems to have lost few aspirants because of his methods. Instead, he built a strong, loyal following who loved and respected their abbot.

The miracles told of Columban multiply, each with a blend of New Testament overtones and Gaelic narrative. Columban restores health, alters death and brings sinners back to Christ. He argues successfully with a bear over the remains of a dead stag whose hide he covets for sandals. He urges his monks to harvest a field during a severe storm and, by placing a brother at each corner of the acreage, he creates an island of sunshine bounded by torrential rains.

Sometimes his miraculous power was combined with earthly wisdom. Once he returned to the monastery to find the fields untended and the monks ill and abed. Calling them to come forth to labor, he brought many to their feet. As soon as they reached the meadow, their sickness vanished. Those who remained in quarters did not recover for several days.

Misfortune now descended on Columban; he would live in its shadow until death rescued him. His peace became subject to politics, and his power was spent in combat with kings.

Sigibert's grandsons now held the thrones in the divided kingdom—Theoderic in Burgundy and Theodebert in Austrasia. Their mother, Brunhilda, resided with Theoderic and sanctioned the dissolute life which he led. Unable to turn his back on this wickedness, Columban remonstrated with Theoderic and exacted a promise of reform. Eventually the old Queen ordered Columban out of the palace, however, and forbade any of her subjects to aid the Luxeuil monks.

Knowing that his brothers were dependent on the neighboring farmers for sustenance, Columban hurried to Theoderic with an appeal. The corrupt monarch feared Columban and sought to placate his anger with a royal repast. In the presence of the servants, the golden goblets were smashed and the gift refused. Theoderic then apologized and asked forgiveness.

The ensuing truce was temporary. Theoderic, urged on by Brunhilda, forced his way into the monastery at Luxeuil, demanding to know why certain portions of the community were closed to visitors.

Columban explained that they were cloistered areas and that Theoderic entered them at his peril. The rash king, though terrified, plunged ahead.

"So be it," said Columban grimly. "Not three years shall pass but you will die and your kingdom will be forfeit."

Theoderic's fear quickened his determination to rid himself of Columban. He found an excuse in an ecclesiastical controversy which plagued the Irish missionaries. The Columban monasteries continued to celebrate Easter according to an ancient Roman reckoning, relying upon the fullness of the moon, regardless of the day of the week. Sunday was now the accepted feast day on the Continent, so Columban was accused of being schismatic in his interpretation.

A synod was convoked to settle the matter. Columban realized in advance that its findings would be prejudiced. He appealed to the synod to deliberate in the spirit of charity, permitting both customs to co-exist.

"Surely there should be room in Gaul for you and us," he pleaded, "as there will be in heaven, if we are worthy. My one request is that you allow us to remain at peace here in the woods, where lie the bones of seventeen of our brothers vho have died."

The appeal failed, as did a famous letter which may never have reached Pope Gregory the Great. In this powerful document, Columban asks what is wrong with celebrating Easter in this fashion. He states that the local bishops could better spend their time reproving the king, or reforming the clergy, or combatting the simony which had placed many of them in office. His letter was probably stopped somewhere short of the Vatican, as were later letters to other popes.

Deportation orders arrived from King Theoderic, and Columban, with some of his original companions, was forced from Luxeuil and sent to Besançon under guard. Here the saint visited the

city jail and secured promises of repentance from
the criminals. He ordered Domoal to pull the
chains from the wall and they came away like
rotten wood. The prisoners fled with Columban
to the Besançon cathedral but found the doors
barred against entry. As a company of soldiers
approached, Columban's prayers opened the por-
tals and then closed them against Theoderic's
troops. After this Columban was left unmolested,
so long as he remained within the city walls.

One day, however, he noted that the road to
Luxeuil was unguarded, so he and his companions
returned to their monastery. The king sent soldiers to remove him, but he was hidden from their
eyes. A second troop found him in church and
dragged him off, apologizing for their unwanted
task.

A long journey across France began for the
Irish monks. The native disciples of Columban
were ordered to remain behind as the others were
led out of the Vosges, across Burgundy and to
the Loire River near Orléans where they boarded
a small ship. En route Columban performed other
miracles, casting out devils and converting a
would-be assassin who tried to run him through
with his lance. A bishop, seeing their condition
in a vision, brought food to their boat, and a
Syrian woman assuaged their hunger on another

occasion. For this favor, her husband's sight was restored.

At Tours, Columban sought permission to go ashore to visit the tomb of St. Martin. Instead, the sailors were commanded to row past the city with all speed. The ship refused to move and drifted to shore. Columban was allowed to make his visit, and he spent the night by the sepulcher. On returning to the ship, he discovered that the few possessions of his monks had been stolen. He addressed St. Martin in prayer, berating him for permitting this to happen to his friends while they were paying homage to Martin's memory. The thieves, groaning under their burden, returned the stolen goods.

Soon they arrived at Nantes, near the mouth of the Loire River. Columban saw his monks board a large vessel and then prepared to follow in a smaller ship. While waiting, he wrote a beautiful letter to his brethren at Luxeuil, exposing his soul to them, counseling them in their daily lives, providing for leadership now that he was gone.

As the ship with the party of monks put to sea, a storm came up and the distraught captain could make no headway. His vessel was beached a few miles from its launching site and withstood all efforts to refloat it. In desperation the captain recalled the story of Jonah and the sailors, so he set the monks ashore. The next tide took his ship to sea.

Now free, Columban led his company back into France, coursing northeast toward the Kingdom of Neustria where Clothaire, a cousin of Theoderic and Theodebert, reigned. The two brothers were preparing for war against each other, and each sought Clothaire as an ally. Columban warned him to remain neutral and he would inherit both kingdoms.

From Neustria he journeyed south to Austrasia and the court of Theodebert. This king, more amiable than his brother, ceded some land near Lake Constance to Columban. Their first mission here, near Tuggen, was razed by the Alamannians, a semi-pagan tribe. The monks built again at Bregenz, a few miles away, and confronted more opposition. The fearless preaching of Gall, however, silenced the enemies of the Church for the moment.

The war edged closer, and Columban advised Theodebert to give up the struggle and enter a monastery. Theodebert refused, bringing a warning that, "if you do not become a cleric by choice, you will become one against your will."

This warning proved prophetic as Theoderic routed his brother's army and forced Theodebert into a monastery. A few days later he was dragged out and executed. Columban felt it wise to move on since his former enemy was now in possession of his land.

As they prepared to depart, Gall became feverish and requested permission to remain behind. Columban, thinking that his old friend feared the arduous retreat, allowed him to stay but punished his supposed disobedience with the mandate that Gall should not say Mass again while Columban lived. In tears, they parted.

Saint Columban was seventy-three years old when he crossed the Alps, fording swollen rivers, brooking cold winds and rocky passages. At last he came to Milan, where King Agilulf ruled the Lombards, another Germanic tribe which had conquered much of Italy. Agilulf's queen, Theodelinda, was a Catholic while Agilulf, himself, was an Arian. However, the king was friendly to Columban, extending him the court's hospitality and even consenting to adopt the Roman Catholic faith if Columban could resolve the dispute regarding Arianism. This heresy denied the nature of Christ as God and was strong among the Christian Lombards, together with the Nestorian heresy which denied the unity of Christ's dual nature.

Encouraged by this opportunity to settle an onerous controversy, Columban wrote a five-thousand-word letter to Pope Boniface IV. The language is rich and colorful, replete with descriptive prose and even a few awkward puns. In the letter he reaffirms the ties of the Irish Church with Rome and recalls some of the earlier disputes about the Easter celebration. He calls upon Boniface to convoke a synod to resolve the present schism. He is even bold enough to remind the Pope of his duty and to challenge him to remove the suspicion current in some quarters about the schismatic sympathies of the Vatican. No reply to this letter has been discovered, but Columban's attempts at reclaiming the Lombards bore fruit within his lifetime. His successors finished the task.

The last chapter in the saint's life occurred at Bobbio, where he moved with his monks to construct his final monastery. Built upon the ruins of a basilica dedicated to St. Peter, this house was famed for its extensive library. The aging abbot helped in the construction, carrying rocks and wooden beams like a young man. He had few months left to enjoy the results of his labor.

In Gaul, King Clothaire had defeated Theoderic and united Austrasia, Neustria and Burgundy as Columban had predicted. The king asked Columban to return to Luxeuil, offering to pay his expenses and give him whatever he requested. The saint gratefully refused the offer but commended his monks at Luxeuil to the king's care.

On November 23rd, 615 A.D., Columban died in Italy. St. Gall, confined to the Alpine monastery which he founded, had a vision of this death and offered a Mass for his abbot, breaking the long penance. Some weeks later, Columban's staff was received by Gall as a symbol of his paternal affection for his former comrade.

The effects of Columban's mission are felt to this day. His name is honored by Catholics in France, Germany, and Italy and by his own countrymen in Ireland. His disciples brought the faith to countless multitudes on the Continent.

When he first asked permission to go abroad, Columban reminded his abbot, Comgall, of Christ's statement: "I have come to cast fire upon the earth, and what will I, but that it be kindled?"

Columban's flame illumined the Christian course of the centuries which follow.

(1095-1148) st. malachy

CHAPTER SIX

"God's wisdom to guide me . . ."

The centuries following Columban's death were, at first, glorious years for the Church. Irish missionaries marched across the Continent of Europe —Fursa, Fiacre, Gilbrien, Rumald in France; Kilian, Colman, Virgilius in Germany; Donatus and Cathaldus in Italy. They were but a few of the hundreds of zealous Irish priests who carried the word of Christ into foreign lands.

At home, too, Catholicism flourished. Ireland's

monastic schools were the envy of the civilized world. Her art and architecture, usually embodying Christian symbolism, reached its zenith. It was an age of golden chalices, brilliantly illuminated manuscripts, and memorable verse. All of this was to change.

Continual raids by the Vikings along the Irish coast from 795 on soon expanded into major invasions. Their success varied, but the invaders did manage to establish themselves in important ports such as Dublin and Limerick. Danes followed the Norsemen, contesting the land with them and with the Irish. Often local Irish chieftains allied themselves with the invaders against a neighbor. At the battle of Clontarf, in 1014, Brian Boru and Malachi finally routed the Northmen, killing seven thousand in a Good Friday battle, thus ending the Viking era.

With the defeat of the Northmen, three powerful Irish families commenced years of bloody struggle for the post of High King of Ireland. The O'Loughlins of Ulster, the O'Connors of Connaught, and the O'Briens of Munster marched and countermarched, winning, losing, advancing, retreating and turning the countryside into one vast battlefield. Roderick O'Connor's ultimate triumph was cut short by the Norman invasion which altered forever the course of Irish history.

Understandably, these ceaseless wars had their effect upon the Catholic Church in Ireland. Some Continental scholars have painted a very gloomy picture of the state of Irish Christianity. While these reports are much exaggerated, there is little doubt that many areas of the country were lax with regard to the Sacraments, careless in some of their canonical interpretations, and corrupt in the appointment of priests, laymen and bishops to choice clerical positions. The situation called for reform. In St. Malachy O'More, the Irish found their reformer.

St. Malachy was born midway between the defeat of the Northmen and the advent of the Normans. His birthplace is uncertain but may have been in County Down. Data on his family is also scarce, although we know that his father held a professor's chair at Armagh and that the boy was raised in this cathedral city. During a trip to Munster in 1102, when Malachy was seven, this teacher-father died, leaving a widow and three children. Malachy's brother, Christian, later earned lasting fame as a devout and kindly abbot. His sister, as we shall see, scandalized her pious brothers by her conduct.

Malachy's mother was careful not to spoil her children and was concerned that they should have, above all else, a fear of the Lord and a love of His commandments. These she inculcated at home while entrusting the boys to the most competent teachers in Armagh. Malachy was a good student; faculty members marked him as obedient, respectful and talented.

Malachy later turned himself over to Imar O'Hagan, a remarkable hermit who dwelt in a cell near the church at Armagh. Imar lived a harsh existence, punishing himself with difficult labors, long hours of prayer, and even self-inflicted physical pain. Malachy adopted this regimen, living near by and enduring the same sufferings. Friends of the young nobleman criticized his stark outlook and tried to lead him away from Imar. From the hermit, however, Malachy learned more than pain. He learned Gregorian chant, advanced theology—and he learned to admire Imar's passion for reform.

Such was Malachy's progress that in 1117 Bishop Cellach of Armagh named him deacon. Malachy was only twenty-two, a year younger than normally required for the office. He tried unsuccessfully to refuse the honor, but, once installed, he plunged earnestly into his work.

One day his sister, whose immoral life was a thorn in Malachy's side, taunted him as he buried a corpse.

"Don't you know that the Bible says, 'Let the dead bury the dead'?"

He turned on her sharply. "You quote Scripture well, but you are ignorant of its spirit." He vowed never to speak to her again.

Bishop Cellach made Malachy his vicar-general and asked him to set his hand to the reform of the diocese. In the bishop's absence, Malachy preached the efficacy of penance, the dignity of matrimony and the proper sequence of the canonical hours. If the people would not come to him, he went to them. When Bishop Cellach returned, he was overjoyed by the improvements Malachy had produced.

The experience convinced Malachy that he needed further training, so he journeyed to Lismore to study under Malchus, a noted canonist who was bishop of Lismore and Waterford. The bishop employed Malachy as an assistant while he pursued his studies.

While Malachy was in Lismore, news reached him of his sister's untimely death. Although he had vowed not to speak to her in life, he now directed his prayers toward her salvation. After many months Malachy stopped praying for her, convinced she must be in heaven. One night, however, she appeared to him in a dream and said that she had eaten nothing in a month, the time of Malachy's last memorial Mass. He began anew and soon had successive dreams in which he saw his sister entering a church dressed at first in black, part-way down the aisle in grey, and, finally, on the altar in white. He interpreted this to mean she had come to rest in Christ.

In 1123, Malachy's uncle, a layman, named his young nephew to succeed him at Bangor. Again Malachy demurred before accepting the post. He gave away all the revenue-producing monastic lands, however, much to the disappointment of his friends and superiors. Bangor, which had been one of Ireland's educational showplaces, had been reduced to ruins by Danish marauders. Malachy rebuilt it to its former glory.

Then, reluctantly, he accepted the bishopric of Down and Connor where conditions were among the worst in Ireland. Bangor remained his headquarters, but Malachy traveled his diocese, preaching to individuals, small crowds or large congregations. For four years he struck firmly and courageously at the barbarous customs, loose morals and dishonest finances of the see. Once again, his efforts were crowned with success.

Then the wars caught up with Bishop Malachy. Conor O'Loughlin, a northern chief, drove through Down and Antrim, evicting the monks of Bangor and leveling their new monastery. Malachy fled to Munster to seek the hospitality of King Cormac McCarthy for his dispossessed community. The previous year, Malachy had sheltered and advised this king while McCarthy was in temporary exile. Grateful for this kindness, Cormac gave Malachy land in Kerry for a new settlement. He added sheep, cattle, money and his own labor in constructing the Iveragh monastery. Malachy had returned to the simple life of a monk, the life he always sought and desired.

Again he was interrupted. Bishop Cellach of Armagh died and named Malachy his successor. Malachy had anticipated this nomination because of a vision in which he was given the crozier of Cellach. But complications arose. It was common practice for the kinsmen of the deceased prelate to elect a replacement. They settled on a man called Murtagh and placed him on the episcopal throne. Malachy refused to press his claim until Malchus, Gilbert of Limerick (the Papal Legate), several bishops, and the kings of Desmond and Lismore insisted that he demand what was rightfully his. The Papal Legate even resorted to a threat of excommunication. Malachy proceeded to Armagh after exacting a promise that he could retire when he had the situation in order.

For two years, Murtagh and Malachy quietly contested the see, although Malachy would not enter the cathedral city for fear of provoking bloodshed. Murtagh died in 1134 but named Niall, brother of Cellach, to succeed him. As Malachy called a meeting to discuss this turn of events, Niall dispatched a party of assassins who lay in waiting on a hill commanding the meeting area. A sudden storm struck the conspirators and lightning killed a dozen of them. The plot failed.

Another narrow escape for Malachy occurred when he answered a summons to a peace conference with a chieftain who intended to murder him. On meeting Malachy, the chieftain repented and became his ally. In the face of this display of power, Niall capitulated but took with him the symbolic Armagh staff and book which to many of the faithful represented authority. Malachy ultimately recovered both objects and reigned for three years as Primate of the Irish Church.

When Malachy returned to Bangor in 1137, he found that both Malchus and Imar O'Hagan were dead. King Cormac and Malachy's brother, Christian, were to follow the next year. Although these loved ones were taken from him, however, Malachy had yet to meet the man who would become his dearest friend.

After dividing the dioceses of Down and Connor into two districts, Malachy rebuilt Bangor as a priory for Canons Regular of St. Augustine and returned to the solitary monastic schedule. Again it was a brief interval, and the next move would find him leaving Ireland.

Papal sanction had never been obtained officially for the sees of Armagh and Cashel, and Malachy determined to visit Innocent II in Rome

to conclude this matter. His brethren opposed the
trip and suggested that he abide by a cast of the
dice. Although refusing to stake his mission on
chance, he was relieved when the dice fell con-
tinually in his favor and his monks stopped ob-
jecting.

With a few companions and a trio of pack animals, Malachy embarked in late 1139 or early
1140. His ship took him first to Scotland where
the group trudged overland to York. Here St.
Waltheof of Wickham presented Malachy with a
rather sorry horse. It is said that by a miracle
the wild, black, bony creature became a white,
docile and magnificent steed which served Malachy many years.

Crossing to France, Malachy led his monks
eastward to an encounter which was to insure his
lasting fame. At Clairvaux he met St. Bernard
who was to become his official biographer. For
a brief time Malachy lived at Clairvaux and was
completely taken by the spirit and rule of the
Cistercian monks. As he proceeded to Rome, a
new intention was in his mind—to request permission of the Pope to resign his bishopric and
live at Clairvaux.

When he arrived at the Vatican, he received
an audience with Innocent II and laid before him
the matter of the Irish sees and his own preference. The Pope promised approval of the sees,

once official documents could be passed, but he denied Malachy's plea for release from his Irish responsibilities. In so doing, Innocent displayed excellent judgement. As a result of his decision the monks at Clairvaux did not gain a colleague, but Ireland herself soon had a Cistercian monastery. To insure this, Malachy left four of his monks with St. Bernard to learn the Cistercian Rule.

When Malachy returned to Bangor, he carried with him an added assignment. Pope Innocent had named him to replace Gilbert as Papal Legate in Ireland. In this new capacity he exerted his usual vigor, traveling throughout the country, making his personality felt in the struggle for reform. He invited St. Bernard to dispatch some French monks to help in the founding of the Cistercian monastery at Mellifont, six miles west of Drogheda. The work progressed slowly, largely due to the failure of the Irish and the French to agree on architectural design. At length Malachy had this new foundation to list among his achievements.

Malachy's miraculous powers received additional tests. He continued to heal the sick and raise the dead to life. His unresolved debate with a heretic ended as the suddenly stricken renegade recanted on his deathbed. He kept two warring armies apart by causing a stream to flood in the dry season, and he cured a nagging housewife

whose tongue, says St. Bernard, "created a solitude whithersoever she came." To secure the release of an imprisoned nobleman, he refused to
eat until King Turlough Mor O'Connor par-
doned the victim. These and other similar hap-
penings are recorded by St. Bernard.

When asked about his preference as to a time
and place for his death, St. Malachy replied that
he would like to expire on All Souls Day in Ireland. And if it could not be Ireland, then he
would like to die at Clairvaux. His wish was close
to fulfillment.

After presiding at a synod on Inishpatrick, off
Skerries, in 1148, Malachy offered to deliver the
official papers on the sees of Armagh and Cashel
to the new Pope, Eugenius III, who was then in
France. His friends again tried to dissuade him,
but Malachy persisted, despite his own premo-
nitions of death.

Two of his disciples begged him to agree in
advance to a proposal they would make. Malachy
assented and then regretted the promise, since it
was that he should return to Ireland. He felt certain that he would never see Erin again. However, when his ship put to sea, it was driven back
upon the land by a strong head wind, and Malachy took this unexpected reversal as fulfillment
of the promise. Then he crossed the Irish Sea for
the last time.

King Stephen of England knew of Malachy's friendship for King David of Scotland, whose son he had cured. Since Stephen suspected David of intrigue, he prevented Malachy from sailing immediately to France. This delay cost the saint a chance to confer with Pope Eugenius, who had left for Rome. So Malachy made his way to St. Bernard at Clairvaux.

His last days were happy ones in the company of Bernard and his exemplary community. After celebrating Mass on the Feast of St. Luke (October 18), Malachy became ill and had to retire to his bed.

The Cistercians vied with one another for the honor of ministering to their guest until Malachy, embarrassed, asked that they lavish less attention upon him.

When the fever became more intense, Malachy requested that he be anointed. He refused the offer to have the Last Sacraments brought to him but left his sickbed and walked to the church to receive them.

Toward evening of All Saints Day, the dying Malachy spoke lucidly to those gathered about his cot.

"I will remember you," he promised, "if such remembrance is permitted. I am certain it will be permitted, for I have believed in God and to him who believes, all things are possible. I have loved

God and I have loved you, and charity never falleth away."

At midnight, Malachy serenely breathed his last.

His burial took place at Clairvaux, but subsequently his skull was exhibited as a relic in the cathedral at Troyes, France. St. Bernard's headbones form a companion piece. The remaining bones of the two saints, though buried separately, are now intermingled with those of three other saints. This was the result of a move by the economically minded Curé of the parish of Ville-sous-la-Ferte where the remains were transferred.

In some quarters, Malachy's principal legacy is the series of prophecies erroneously attributed to him. These deal with the fate of the Church in Ireland and with cryptic predictions as to the identity of future popes. Most Catholics should remember him as did St. Bernard in advising Eugenius III on the conduct of his office:

"Study the life and follow the example of St. Malachy, and all will be well."

(1128-1180) St. LauRence O'toole

CHAPTER SEVEN

"Christ to shield me today . . ."

Like his contemporary, St. Malachy, St. Laurence O'Toole died in France and was buried in alien soil, the last of Ireland's canonized saints until the 20th century. His life spanned the most critical events in Ireland's history.

Born Lorcan Ua Tuathail, Laurence is best known by his anglicized name. Even this has its story. His parents intended to christen him Conor O'Toole, but as the baptismal party was

en route to the church a holy man stopped them
and proclaimed that the child should be named
Laurence. At the cathedral the stranger repeated
his prophecy to the waiting father. Impressed
with the omen, the family instructed the Bishop
of Kildare to make the change.

Scarcely a day's march from Dublin, where the
infant would one day earn lasting fame, lay the
little village of Castledermot. Here Laurence was
born to Murtagh, chieftain of the Hy-Murray,
and Inian Ivrien, daughter of O'Byrne, a neighboring prince. Laurence was greatly influ-
enced by his mother and tried sincerely to imitate
her charity and devotion. Even at an early age
he would slip away, seek some quiet niche, and
spend hours in prayer and meditation. He was a
bright student, educated by bardic tutors who
frequented the courts.

When Laurence was ten years old, his father
fought unsuccessfully against the army of the terrible Dermot MacMurrogh. His kingdom overrun and his clansmen in retreat, Murtagh
O'Toole sued for peace. One of the conditions
of the surrender was the gift of a daughter to be
the bride of MacMurrogh and the deliverance of
Laurence as a hostage.

In ordinary circumstances, the youthful cap-
tive could have expected decent treatment and
considerable freedom. Under the cruel Mac-

Murrogh, however, Laurence fared worse than any slave. For two years he toiled in the sterile, rocky region around Ferns. Already he was learning to endure suffering patiently and in silence.

Eventually Murtagh heard of this brutal treatment. Unable to attack MacMurrogh directly, he did manage to capture a dozen of his officers who had strayed into Murray territory. In exchange for their release, he demanded that MacMurrogh deliver his son to the Bishop of Glendalough. Reluctantly, MacMurrogh agreed to the transfer. Laurence was sent to St. Kevin's ancient monastery above the twin lakes in Wicklow.

His father hurried to him. Impressed by the kindness of the monks and grateful for his son's escape, the O'Toole chieftain vowed that one of his four sons should be dedicated to the service of the Church. He offered to cast lots to decide among them. At this proposal, Laurence laughed.

"There is no need to cast lots, father," he declared. "For many months I have intended to become a priest."

Murtagh blessed his son and then left him at Glendalough to pursue his vocation. The growth from novice to monk was a severe test of faith and endurance. The Rule of St. Benedict was strict, but to Laurence, who had suffered the years of hardship at Ferns, it was filled with spiritual solace. At twenty-five, he was chosen to lead the community as its abbot. Youth alone prevented him from being consecrated a bishop.

The responsibility of being abbot was a staggering challenge for such a young man. Laurence was required to preside over men much older than himself, to guide them spiritually, and provide for them materially. Despite his youth, Laurence came to be regarded by the other monks as a kindly father, and his counsel was praised as being worthy of men twice his age. Even neighboring princes came to consult this "oracle of Glendalough."

When famine struck, Laurence used not only the monastic resources but his own inheritance from his father to relieve the hunger of the poor. When bandits and highwaymen infested the Wicklow mountains and made the roads unsafe for travel, Laurence went among them, gently chastizing them for their conduct and converting many to a Christian life.

In 1161, Gregory, the first bishop of Dublin, died and the see fell vacant. To the native Irish, Dublin was virtually a foreign city. Danes made up a large percentage of the population and Norse traditions dominated the culture. Its citizens were sailors and merchants who looked to Britain as their seat of government. This course extended to religious authority. Gregory had been consecrated in England, for Dublin bishops owed allegiance to Canterbury.

Saint Laurence started a new and short-lived trend. He was the first and the last Dublin bishop to be consecrated in Ireland for many centuries. Gelasius, who had succeeded Malachy at Armagh, performed the ceremony.

Chroniclers describe Laurence as tall, graceful and dignified, but he was no fragile courtier. On assuming responsibility for the diocese, he reviewed the scattered population subject to him and investigated the state of his clergy. The need for reform was apparent, so Laurence undertook it fearlessly. His priests, particularly those in higher offices, were required to abide by stricter rules. Laurence, himself, donned the religious habit of the Augustinians, ate in their refectory, observed their periods of silence, and assisted at midnight office.

From the pulpit and in the market place, Laurence preached against error and laxity. He brought the poor of Dublin to share his table and served them personally. Along the coast, from Meath to Wexford, he journeyed, visiting the Danish fishing villages of Wicklow. His people of mixed ancestry began to appreciate his efforts and obey his decrees.

Thomas, a nephew of Laurence O'Toole, had become abbot of Glendalough. Whenever Lau-

rence felt the need of solitude or whenever he
wished to pray over some difficult problem, he
would hasten to Glendalough and climb to the
rock-hewn cave in the hillside. Here, in St.
Kevin's Sanctuary, he spent his few peaceful moments.

Even in crowded Dublin he lived a life of de-
nial. Beneath his episcopal robes he wore a hair
shirt. He abstained from meat, and on Fridays he
ate only bread and water. At night he slept little
but knelt in the darkness, praying. In addition to
his duties as bishop, Laurence preached, lectured,
instructed children, reformed monasteries and
convents, visited the sick, and even begged for
the poor and for the orphans in a near-by asy-
lum. New churches all over Dublin gave tangi-
ble evidence of this religious renaissance. A
trained musician, Laurence also raised Gregorian
Chant to its proper place in the liturgy.

When Laurence was forty-two, Dermot Mac-
Murrogh cast his contrary shadow across the
bishop's path once more. Driven from Ireland by
the combined forces of his many enemies, the
hated MacMurrogh appealed to King Henry II
of England for help in regaining his kingdom.
The king was fighting in Aquitaine at the time
but gave MacMurrogh a letter permitting him to
enlist the support of any English barons who
might be interested. The Irish chieftain found

such an adventurer in Richard de Clare, Earl of Pembroke, nicknamed "Strongbow." On the heels of some smaller probing attacks, Strongbow landed at Waterford in 1170 and subdued Leinster with his modest but seasoned regiments. Then he marched on Dublin.

Bishop Laurence met the invaders and tried to dissuade them from battle. While he was on this mission, the Normans breached the city's defenses and slaughtered its citizens. Laurence raced back to tend the wounded and protect the survivors from further massacre.

Belatedly, the Irish began to organize a counterattack. Across the beleaguered island many minor skirmishes occurred and the Irish won their share of them. In 1171 King Henry crossed the Irish Channel to substantiate his claim to Ireland and prevent his barons from appropriating the territory for themselves. When he returned to London, he attempted to recall Strongbow, but the Earl delayed and soon was pinned within the walls of Dublin by the combined Irish armies under the vacillating Rory O'Connor.

Again, Laurence was chosen as intermediary between the vastly superior Irish force and the caged Normans. Strongbow was desperate, and his desperation led to a daring assault upon the surrounding army. Unfortunately for the Irish, Rory O'Connor was only a fair commander and

his troops had never faced such disciplined soldiers. Strongbow broke their ranks and sent them
reeling. The rout was unexpected and complete
and, despite later English reverses, it sealed the
fate of Ireland.

While consolidating the military and political
gains, the Normans also decided to reorganize the
Irish Church under English authority. Armed
with the historic and controversial Papal Bull of
Adrian IV, they convoked a synod at Cashel in
1172. Although the bull—an official Vatican letter—had been secured seventeen years earlier
from Pope Adrian, an Englishman, Henry was
only now making use of its power. The bull sanctioned Henry's intention of invading Ireland for
the purpose of reforming the Church, for even
the Vatican had heard grossly exaggerated tales
of corruption in Ireland. Now the deed was done,
and Henry's action seemingly carried the benediction of Rome.

The decisions of the Synod of Cashel recog-
nized Britain's dominant role in Irish ecclesiastical matters. In a few short centuries this transfer
would produce calamitous effects as King Henry
VIII broke with the Church of Rome. At
the moment, however, the change was accepted
rather calmly by the clergy around Dublin. Alexander III, the current Pope, gave his approval
and Bishop Laurence concurred.

From this time forth, Laurence was to spend much of his time as ambassador between the Irish princes and the English king. He fared well with Strongbow, Earl of Pembroke. Eva, the Earl's wife, was a niece of the O'Tooles. When the Earl died in 1176, Laurence was at his side and later conducted the funeral services.

The year before Strongbow's death, Laurence nearly lost his own life. On a diplomatic mission to Windsor Castle to negotiate a treaty between King Henry and Rory O'Connor, the Bishop stopped at Canterbury and spent the night in prayer before the altar-shrine of the newly-martyred Thomas à Becket. The next morning, as Laurence was saying Mass, a maniac darted from the shadows of the cathedral and struck him down with a heavy club. The blow should have killed him, but Laurence recovered quickly and continued with the Mass. An examination of the saint's skull centuries later clearly showed the imprint of the savage stroke.

In 1179, the Third General Council of the Lateran was held in Rome. Among the delegates were Bishop Laurence and five other Irish bishops. Before receiving permission to attend, the six prelates had to promise King Henry that they would say nothing to the Pope which would prejudice the English position in Ireland.

In a private audience with the Pope, Laurence

begged that effective measures be taken in his homeland to correct disorders and free the Church from civil strife. Alexander III agreed to do what he could, and he displayed his pleasure with Laurence by naming him his Papal Legate in Ireland. He also confirmed all of the rights and privileges of the Dublin see and added Ferns, Glendalough, Kildare, Leighlin and Ossory to Laurence's jurisdiction.

Taking his new responsibility seriously, Laurence returned to Ireland and resolutely purged his clergy of abuses which were beginning to reappear in the wake of the invasion. One hundred and forty offenders were sent to Rome to seek forgiveness. Among them were many new priests, assigned under the Norman administration. When this forthright display of power was reported to King Henry, he grew fearful that another Becket had arisen. Perhaps he felt Laurence had broken his promise in Rome, or he may have been hurt because the papal appointment had been made without his sanction.

In any event, when Laurence arrived in England in 1180 to intercede for Rory O'Connor with the King, Henry barred his return to Ireland. For three weeks, Laurence was detained at Abingdon. Impatient to continue his work, he sought out King Henry and learned that the

English sovereign had sailed to Normandy. Laurence immediately took passage for France.

Landing near Le Tréport, at a place still called Saint-Laurent, Laurence dispatched another message to his king, begging leave to return to Dublin. Moved by the petition, Henry lifted the ban. But the order came too late.

As Laurence approached the Abbey of the Canons Regular of St. Victor at Eu, he predicted that this would be his final resting place. He was stricken with a fever and sought shelter in the monastery. Here he lingered but a few days.

While still conscious, he was asked about making a will. Laurence smiled. "God knows I have not a penny in the world," he said.

His last words were about his countrymen:

"Ah, foolish and senseless people, what will become of you now? Who will defend you? Who will relieve your sorrow?"

On Friday, November 14, he died. A holy man at Christ Church in Dublin witnessed the death in a vision and announced it to the Irish people days before the fact could be verified.

Saint Laurence O'Toole was laid to rest in France. His principal relics remain in a crypt at Notre Dame Church in Eu, although one large relic is preserved in a parish dedicated to the saint, near North Strand, Dublin.

Forty-five years later, in 1225, the miracles attributed to Bishop Laurence were authenticated and the process of canonization was completed. Saint Laurence closed out a Gaelic era which could never be recaptured.

(1629 - 1681) st. oliver plunkett

CHAPTER EIGHT

"Against every cruel merciless power that may oppose my body and soul . . ."

The five hundred years separating Laurence O'Toole and Oliver Plunkett were agonizing years for Ireland and dismal ones for her Church. The nation suffered military reverses, political reprisals and, finally, religious persecution.

In 1534, King Henry VIII of England passed the Act of Supremacy, severing relations with

Rome and declaring himself head of the Catholic
Church in England—and in Ireland. Suppression
of the monasteries followed, then heavy fines
against Catholics, restrictions on their devotion
and their education, and, sometimes, death to
those who resisted. Queen Elizabeth I accelerated
the cruelties, and the advent of the Stuart kings
did nothing to lessen the devastation. Catholic
landowners were disinherited; their children were
forbidden to attend schools at home or abroad;
their priests were hunted into the hills and bogs
and murdered when discovered.

Ireland did not submit quietly. Under Hugh
O'Neill and Red Hugh O'Donnell they conquered invading armies for six years before the
two leaders fled to the Continent in 1607. Thirty-
four years later a new O'Neill—Owen Roe—
headed the Rebellion of 1641 and defeated a
succession of English generals sent against him.
At Kilkenny, in 1642, the Irish and Anglo-
Irish united against the English for a brief return to power. The Confederation did not last,
however, and the Irish were crushed by Cromwell.

In 1629, at Loughcrew, County Meath, Oliver Plunkett was ushered into this stormy era.
His mother was related to the Earls of Roscom-
mon, and his father's family was one of the most
renowned of the Anglo-Irish houses. The Earl of

Fingall, Lord Louth, Lord Dunsany and Lord Rathmore were all kinsmen, and Sir Nicholas Plunkett, a cousin, was Ireland's most famous attorney. Another cousin, Patrick Plunkett, was Abbot of St. Mary's, Dublin, and later became Bishop of Ardagh and of Meath. To this Cistercian prelate was given the responsibility of educating young Oliver.

Until he was sixteen, Oliver devoted himself to his studies, impressing his cousin with his spiritual qualities and convincing him that the boy had a vocation to the priesthood. When Father Peter Scarampo, papal envoy to Ireland, was leaving Dublin in 1645 to return to Rome with his report on Church conditions, Bishop Plunkett persuaded him to take young Oliver with him.

After escaping from a British privateer in the Channel and from bandits in the Low Countries, Father Scarampo and his youthful companion arrived in the Rome of Pope Innocent X. Sponsored by the papal envoy, Oliver lived in the Irish College founded by Cardinal Ludovisi and attended the Roman College of the Society of Jesus. Here, under the Jesuits, he compiled a brilliant academic record in philosophy, theology and mathematics. This success continued at the University—La Sapienza—where he graduated with honors in Law, both civil and canon.

Father Scarampo maintained the student out

of his own meager purse, and Oliver, in return, later assisted another student. He always cherished his collegiate days, and from his limited income he purchased a vineyard for the Irish College.

In the summer of 1654, Oliver Plunkett was ordained. This usually meant a return to Ireland, but Cromwell was then putting the country to the sword, so Oliver petitioned to remain in Rome until tensions should abate. He was given a theological post at the Missionary College of the Congregation of the Propagation of the Faith. While teaching here, he acted as agent for the Irish bishops to the Vatican and used every opportunity to plead the cause of Ireland.

Rome was a fascinating city, and Oliver lived there during some of its most interesting days. Though a time of political unrest, it was an era of intellectual renaissance. The Irish professor became an expert in theology, attracting prominent theologians and laymen to sit in discussion with him. Despite this active career, Oliver spent considerable time in prayer, pilgrimage, and penance. Without realizing it, he was preparing himself for the trials just ahead.

News from Ireland reached him through papal nuncios in Paris and Brussels, from exiled priests and bishops, and from a variety of other sources. All of the news was bad. Cromwell's death did little to soften the English persecution. Three Irish bishops were executed and the remainder of the hierarchy were under sentence of death or exile. Only two prelates remained free in Ireland. One was old and infirm, and the other, Patrick Plunkett of Ardagh, was in hiding. There was danger of a total collapse of Church authority, so Pope Clement IX named four new bishops to take up their posts. In the wake of these appointments, the exiled Archbishop of Armagh died, and this foremost see in Ireland became vacant. Many candidates were suggested to Pope Clement, but he remarked, "Why should we look about when the best choice is right before our eyes in Rome?" Oliver Plunkett was returned to Ireland, after twenty-five years, as the Archbishop of Armagh and the successor to St. Patrick.

Because of the fierce English bias against Rome, Oliver traveled to Ghent, Belgium, to be consecrated and then sailed to London where he was welcomed hospitably by the Catholic wife of King Charles II. For several weeks he remained in London, receiving tours of the capital, briefings on the situation of the Church, and meeting prominent persons with whom he might plead for the mitigation of anti-Catholic laws in Ireland.

In March of 1670, he assumed leadership of the See of Armagh. This province consisted of eleven dioceses, only one of which had a bishop.

With a remarkable display of organization, patience and endurance, the new Archbishop set about to dispel dissension, consolidate authority, and strengthen the faith of the oppressed. It was a formidable assignment.

For the first few months after his return, he had to travel about disguised as one "Captain Brown," complete with wig, sword and pistols, because the priest-hunters were on his trail. His bed was straw and he was often without shelter. His food was oaten bread and porridge. During his reign he rarely had money, and this small amount was exhausted by the demands of his office. One of the principal expenses was his frequent and faithful correspondence with Rome. For fifteen months he lived in the wilds, tracked by enemies, buffeted by wind, snow and hail, tormented by physical ailments.

Despite this, he managed to confirm nearly fifty thousand Catholics during the first four years of his ministry. His ordinations were frequent, though secret, and he convoked several synods. Among the projects most dear to him was the foundation of a high school at Drogheda, during a brief period of peace and relative religious tolerance. He brought in the Jesuits to staff the school which was attended by 150 boys, a third of them from Protestant families. He even promoted missionary activity in the Scottish Hebrides.

Although he was no politician, Archbishop Plunkett maintained excellent relations with Lord Berkeley, English Viceroy to Ireland in the early years of his episcopacy, and with the Earl of Essex who succeeded Berkeley. With Protestant bishops, too, he was in good repute, and his superiors in Rome were heartened by his progress. Unfortunately, he made enemies among his own clergy.

An early dispute between Oliver and Bishop Talbot regarding the primacy of Armagh over Dublin resulted in Armagh's being sustained, but bad feelings lingered. On another occasion the Archbishop was called in to settle a dispute between the Franciscans and the Dominicans regarding territorial jurisdiction. When he decided in favor of the Dominicans, he earned the enmity of a segment of the Franciscans.

An intervention in secular matters also came back to haunt him. During these penal days, outlaws called "Tories" or "Rapparees" infested the outlying districts. They ranged from patriotic dissenters to murdering thieves. In either case, they were a plague to the English Viceroy who asked Archbishop Plunkett to use his influence to stop their depredations. In the Ulster mountains, Oliver met with fifteen of the Tory leaders and ar-

ranged safe conduct for them to France. Since
the Tories had much popular support, including
quiet clerical approbation, this act was severely
criticized as surrendering to the enemy. The
Archbishop's motives, of course, were to settle
conditions in his see, so that religion would have
a chance to prosper.

All things, it seems, conspired against him. Circumstances were ripe for a new and violent out-
break of anti-Catholic feeling. Massacres of Irish
Protestants in the Rising of 1641 were not for-
gotten, and the Great London Fire of 1666 was
falsely, but loudly, laid at the door of the Catholics. Rumors that Charles II was secretly converted to Catholicism disturbed his subjects,
already resentful of his Catholic wife and fearful
of his brother and heir, the Duke of York, also
a Catholic.

Into this explosive situation stepped an incredible character named Titus Oates. A renegade
Catholic, twice expelled from Jesuit seminaries,
this Anglican clergyman concocted the so-called
"Popish Plot" which included claims that the
King was to be assassinated and the Protestants
massacred. The Pope, with the help of the French,
was to seize England and the Jesuits were to be
placed in control of the nation's military forces.
So hysterical was the prevalent anti-Catholic sen-
timent that this fantastic tale was believed. Titus

Oates was hailed as "the Savior of the Nation" and the public hatred of "Papists" spread like a disease.

Lord Shaftesbury, leader of the Opposition to King Charles II, seized the opportunity to discredit the monarch and reduce the possibility of a Catholic succession by perpetuating and expanding the Oates myth. He raised the issue to a fever pitch, resulting in the trial and execution of many Catholics, including five English Jesuits. His malevolence now spread to Ireland where it was to engulf the nation's Primate, the Archbishop of Armagh.

On the 6th of December, 1679, Archbishop Plunkett was confined to Dublin Castle on an unspecified charge. Here he lingered until the following July when he was transferred to Dundalk for trial. Without knowledge of the alleged crimes or of his accusers, the Archbishop had no opportunity to assemble a defense. He heard himself charged with treasonable acts against the Crown, but the State could not produce its prime witnesses, two apostate priests named Mac-Moyer and Murphy. MacMoyer finally appeared, drunk, and said Murphy could not be found. So black was the character of the witnesses that even the unsympathetic jury could not credit them. Plunkett was acquitted. All that now remained was for him to fulfill the law by appearing at three consecutive Assizes and the charge would be wiped from the books.

However, Lord Shaftesbury was not to be cheated so easily. He contrived to have the Archbishop brought to London in October, ten months after his initial arrest. Here he was confined in infamous Newgate Prison, where filth and disease abounded, where rats fought for every scrap of food, where water turned stagnant and the dead mingled with the living. As an added insult, the prisoners had to pay for what they used, even including the leg irons with which they were chained to the dank walls. Blessed Oliver was denied the company of his servant, James Mc-Kenna, or the services of a priest or the opportunity to say Mass.

When he was released on May fifth, he edged through a hostile mob to Westminster Hall to hear the criminal charges read for the first time. He was accused of being the leader of a Popish Plot in Ireland, with recruiting troops, maintaining liaison with the French, spying, and a variety of related offenses which would be spelled out in the trial. Plunkett protested the change of venue and this was denied. He explained that he had been cleared of similar charges in Dundalk, but the court contended that the trial there had never actually occurred. He asked for time to gather witnesses and documents from Ireland and was granted five weeks. In view of the difficulty of travel, both to Ireland and in Ireland, these thirty-five days would not suffice. Oliver's plea for an extension was turned down.

Several other untoward incidents hurt the Archbishop's case. His cousin, the skilled attorney Nicholas Plunkett, died before he could be summoned to aid. Perhaps even more damaging was the fact that the Archbishop's arraignment and trial were held almost simultaneously with those of Edward Fitzharris, a pathetic pawn in a political-religious feud. Fitzharris had been employed as a casual and inept spy by friends of the Catholic Queen. When he couldn't come up with anything of interest, he began to manufacture evidence. For this he was arrested and lodged in Newgate. Here Shaftesbury visited him and tried to get the simple fellow to testify to the existence of the Popish Plot. Before he could carry out the design, the King intervened, keeping Fitzharris incommunicado. Eventually Fitzharris was tried and hanged without being able to involve the King and his family. However, he distracted so much attention from the Archbishop, while exciting the bloodthirsty populace, that he helped bring Oliver Plunkett to a fate which the Archbishop *might* have escaped.

When the trial opened on June eighth, Plunkett was without witnesses. The documents he had hoped to obtain in Ireland, testifying to the corrupt character of his accusers, were held up in a legal tangle. He was allowed no defense counsel, no challenges of the unfriendly jury, and no statement of specific charges. The justices and attorneys for the prosecution ranged from talented to incompetent, but all were united in their feelings against the Catholic religion. As it turned out, it was on his faith, not his patriotism, that the Archbishop was judged.

Nine witnesses appeared against Blessed Oliver. Four of them were apostate priests. Well-coached by Lord Shaftesbury and his agent in charge of gathering evidence, William Hetherington, the witnesses recited tales of intrigue and conspiracy. When they faltered, one of the court attorneys or justices helped them out. Every act of the Archbishop was turned against him, and, when they could not produce a half-truth, they created a complete lie. The impoverished prelate heard himself accused of extorting money from his priests to pay the costs of arms and ammunition. The parish census was characterized as a recruitment capable of producing 60,000 troops from Ulster. Archbishop Plunkett's dealings with the Rapparees were interpreted as a scheme to contact the French, and his dispute with Bishop Talbot was resurrected as proof that he had received his post from Rome in order to lead an insurrection. Two witnesses insisted, despite Plunkett's demand for proof, that the Archbishop toured the Irish ports and selected Carlingford as the best site for a landing of French or Spanish invaders. This port, incidentally, made an almost impossible landing area, but the facts did not matter in this mockery of a trial.

During the cross-examination by the Archbishop, he was often cut short by the judges. Moreover, the attorneys for the prosecution were allowed to coach the witnesses. The record of the trial is full of illegalities by court officers who knew better. Yet they played to the noisy crowd, drawing cheers and applause.

Archbishop Plunkett insisted on his innocence, asking the witnesses why they had not come forward before if they had treasonable evidence, and protesting the obvious contradictions in the garbled testimony. One witness—Edmond Murphy, an excommunicated priest who was a murder suspect—repented and gave such a weak deposition that he was dismissed and imprisoned.

Only one witness appeared for the Archbishop, and he was summoned at the eleventh hour by friends rather than by Oliver. His contribution was a simple declaration that he knew of nothing evil that the Archbishop had done but knew of much good. On that note the trial concluded.

Sir Francis Pemberton, the Lord Chief Justice,

neatly packaged the prejudice in his rebuke of the
defendant's final plea:

> "Look you, Mr. Plunkett, you have been here in-
> dicted of a very great and heinous crime, the greatest
> and most heinous of all crimes, and that is, high
> treason; and truly yours is treason of the highest na-
> ture. It is a treason in truth against God and your
> king, and the country where you lived. You have
> done as much as you could to dishonour our God in
> this case; for the bottom of your treason was your
> setting up of your false religion, than which there is
> not anything more displeasing to God, or more perni-
> cious to mankind in the world. A religion that is ten
> times worse than all the heathenish superstitions; the
> most dishonourable and derogatory to God and his
> glory, of all religions or pretended religions whatso-
> ever, for it undertakes to dispense with God's laws,
> and to pardon the breach of them. So that certainly
> a greater crime there cannot be committed against
> God, than for a man to endeavour the propagation
> of that religion. . . ."

The jury deliberated only fifteen minutes before bringing in a verdict of guilty. On hearing
the foreman, Plunkett said, *"Deo gratias*, God be
thanked."

Seventeen days of life were left to the Archbishop, for his sentence of death was summarily
pronounced. Too late his witnesses arrived from
Ireland. Too late Essex appealed to King Charles
for clemency. Throughout the "Popish" trials,

the English King had been afraid to provoke trouble by intervening. Like Pilate, he washed his hands of the affair, stating, "Let the blood lie on them that condemn them, for God knows I sign [the orders of execution] with tears in my eyes."

Among the consolations in the Archbishop's last days were the kindnesses of the English Catholics, the company of his devoted servant, James McKenna, the ministrations of Father Maurus Corker, Newgate's chaplain, and the privilege of saying Mass. All of these favors were purchased at a price. Supporters in Rome and on the Continent worked toward his release, but all attempts failed. On the first of July he was tied to a wooden hurdle and dragged to his place of execution at Tyburn.

In his speech from the scaffold, Archbishop Plunkett reiterated his protests against the trial and restated his innocence. He also forgave his enemies, made an Act of Contrition and asked the Blessed Virgin, the holy angels and saints to intercede for him. As the hangman knotted the rope around his neck he repeated fervently, "Into Thy hands, O Lord, I commend my spirit. Lord Jesus, receive my soul."

He was hung, his entrails cut out and burned, his body quartered, and his head severed and thrust into the blaze.

The very next day the Popish Plot collapsed

as Lord Shaftesbury was imprisoned by the King. Several of the witnesses met similar fates, and all of them were haunted by their conduct. Hugh Duffy, one of the apostate friars, spent the next forty years of his life as a bandit, appearing at last before Archbishop McMahon of Armagh, to confess and beg forgiveness. Without speaking, the Archbishop opened a shrine in his room and displayed its contents to the penitent man. Duffy fainted on seeing the severed head of Oliver Plunkett, preserved as a relic. The head is now permanently exposed at St. Peter's Church in Drogheda.

Two hundred years after the execution of Archbishop Oliver Plunkett, the first steps toward his beatification were taken. Investigation of the martyr's character and conduct earned him the preliminary appellation of "Blessed." In 1975, the title of "Saint" was formally conferred, recognizing the brightest name in Christendom during the terrible Penal Days.

(1787-1841) mother catherine mcauley

CHAPTER NINE

"Christ in every eye that sees me . . ."

The legacy of St. Brigid produced holy Irish women in every century, from Ethna, the mystic child, to Edel Quinn, a great lay missionary of our time who spread membership in the Legion of Mary across the African continent. No century was more fruitful than the eighteenth century in Ireland.

In a land struggling to be free of religious suppression and persecution, Irish women moved beside the statesmen and the soldiers. They demonstrated the same courage and determination, coupled with a charity and perseverance which ultimately conquered. They nursed the sick to health, dragged the poor up from the slums, and introduced schools to a people to whom education was forbidden. In accomplishing these things, they won the eternal love of their countrymen and the respect of their enemies. They shattered the spiritual and intellectual bonds of Ireland.

Nano Nagle of Cork was one of these. From clandestine learning at the feet of a "hedge" schoolmaster to the finest schools in Paris she progressed, until her father's death in 1746 brought her back to Ireland. An act of charity performed by her sister, Ann, just before Ann's death, left a deep impression on Nano. She entered a French convent, then left it, following her inspiration to serve Ireland. Using her own limited funds and whatever she could borrow, Nano established elementary schools in her native Cork, bringing the Ursulines in to staff them. Still this did not satisfy her desire to alleviate the sufferings of the poor. Her foundation of the Presentation Sisters provided for that charitable undertaking. Nano's death in 1784 preceded by three years the birth of two more foundresses.

The first of these, Mother Mary Aikenhead, was a fellow Corkonian who was chosen by her bishop to head a new community of sisters to work among the poor. These became the Irish Sisters of Charity with twelve convents in Ireland and others in England and Australia during the lifetime of Mother Aikenhead. Despite a spinal condition which invalided her, the foundress humbly and courageously guided her congregation for forty years. When she died, the coffin of this "Queen of Beggars" was carried through the streets by the poor.

Catherine McAuley was also born in 1787, but her home was a fashionable Georgian mansion at Drumcondra, a suburb of Dublin. Ireland's capital city was then a thriving metropolis having the usual mixture of slums and sophistication. Nowhere was Catholicism more out of favor. Priests were no longer hunted down, nor were monasteries sacked and destroyed. However, the legal prohibitions against Catholics had been relaxed very little, and the years had given the Church no time to rebuild and re-educate. Moreover, this religion was despised by the aristocracy as something base and vulgar.

James McAuley, Catherine's father, was an exception. Wealthy and respected, he lived as an exemplary Catholic gentleman. One of his constant concerns was for the poor of Dublin to

whom he gave clothes, food and medicine. They
came to his home, and he sat with them on the
expansive lawn, instructing them in the Catholic
faith. While this impressed the young Catherine,
it found Mrs. McAuley cool and uncomprehend-
ing.

Although she had little appreciation of her husband's attentions to the poor, Eleanor McAuley
was a good mother to Catherine, her sister, Mary,
and her brother, James. She made them conscious of the rights of others and of their own
obligations. Her social ambition, however, caused
her to neglect the children's spiritual training
after the early death of her husband.

Catherine was seven when her father died. The
family was forced to sell the Drumcondra home
and move into Dublin. Here, four years later,
Eleanor McAuley died, reconciled to Catholicism but remorseful because she had failed to
rear her children in that faith. The three orphans
were adopted by relatives, first by a Dr. Conway
and then, after the Conway fortunes lapsed, by
Mr. and Mrs. Armstrong.

The Armstrongs were decent, charitable people, but their sincere and rigid Protestantism led
James and Mary into the same beliefs. Catherine
refused to attend their church because she was
not convinced theirs was the true religion. She
remembered the kindly character of her Catholic

father. Mr. Armstrong agreed to let her read through his library in order to discover the truth. The privilege had a reverse effect. By the time Catherine was sixteen, she had read herself back into the Catholic faith. As she explained to her foster-father, the example of the Catholic martyrs impressed her much more than that of their Protestant counterparts.

Financial reverses caused another move for Catherine. After business conditions impoverished the Armstrongs, a distant relative named Callahan asked to adopt the beautiful and lively girl. Reluctantly, the Armstrongs parted with her, for though they were poor and though they disagreed with Catherine on religious principles, they still loved her. Her new parents loved her, too, and brought her to Coolock House, their manor near Dublin.

During a shopping trip in Dublin, Catherine slipped away to a small chapel where she met Father Murray, later Archbishop of Dublin. To him she told her desire to be a Catholic. This was the first of many visits she managed, resulting in her receiving First Communion and probably Confirmation. All of this was done without her guardians' knowledge.

The Callahans were distressed when Catherine later told them what she had done. They continued to shower affection on her but tried to discourage her from practicing her religion. They provided no way for her to travel the nine miles to Mass on Sunday, and the household menu made no provision for days on which Catherine had to fast or abstain.

She was not allowed to bring religious articles into the house. The Callahans made it difficult for her to meet Father Murray or any other priest. Often visitors would attack the Catholic Church in Catherine's presence, but her spirited defense soon drove back the assailants. Eventually, when the Callahans realized that Catherine was sincere and determined, they became more tolerant.

The next twenty years are often referred to as the "hidden life" of Mother McAuley. She worked among the poor of the neighborhood, using her own allowance to purchase food and clothing for them. She became a rallying point for the indigent Irish as had her father before her.

Mrs. Callahan was stricken with an illness which kept her bed-ridden for two years. During this period Catherine was her constant companion, ministering to her needs and reading to her to keep her entertained. When her foster-mother inquired about Catholicism, Catherine was delighted. She began to instruct her and saw her converted before death.

Mr. Callahan was much grieved by his wife's

death and survived her by two scant years. During that time he, too, became a Catholic. He lived to thank Catherine for the joy her faith had brought into their lives.

He asked Catherine what she would do if she had any financial means and the girl said that she would spend it in caring for the poor. The reply pleased Callahan. "If you possess wealth, Catherine," he said, "you will do good with it." When he died, his entire estate passed into her hands. Thirty thousand pounds, several insurance policies, the magnificent house and its exquisite furnishings—all became the property of the adopted child, now a mature woman of thirty-five.

Catherine's brother and sister had a number of ideas on how the money should be spent, but Catherine ignored material comforts for the goal she set herself. She absolved the estate's debtors and increased her work among the poor. Down into the slums she traveled, carrying food and clothing. She visited hospitals and instructed working girls who came to her home.

In July of 1824, she purchased a site on Lower Baggot Street, a fashionable Dublin suburb, and ordered the construction of a boarding school for girls. Later she sold Coolock House, moved to Lower Baggot Street, and gathered around her women who had ideas like her own. At the time she had no intention of founding a religious congregation, but the new structure strangely took the shape of a convent. Here the poor were always welcome. In addition to religious training, there were lessons in sewing, cooking and keeping house. On Christmas each year, Catherine played host to the poor children of Dublin. The great Catholic statesman, Daniel O'Connell, was a perennial honored guest. Catherine was driven to do more and more for the unfortunate, especially homeless and fugitive girls.

Her brother James, a practicing physician in Dublin after duty as an army surgeon, and her sister Mary, married to a physician named Dr. William McAuley, both urged Catherine to forget this demanding and humiliating existence and marry a major who was courting her. She declined and continued her work.

Among Catherine's later converts were her sister and her sister's children. When Dr. William McAuley learned that Catherine had converted his wife to Catholicism before her death, he was furious and threatened Catherine's life with his sword. She fled his house. Later the doctor regretted his action and even expressed a desire to see a priest on his deathbed. His five children were given over to Catherine to raise. Tuberculosis, which had killed the parents, also ravaged their children. Two daughters, who became nuns under Mother Catherine McAuley, died while very young.

By this time the home was well established and the staff lived pretty much as a religious community. They began calling each other "Sister" in jest and then in earnest. Archbishop Murray, who had been "Father Murray" when he had instructed Catherine in the faith, permitted them to assume a simple black dress and suggested that they select a name for their institute. Catherine, who had long been attracted by the ancient Order of Our Lady of Mercy founded by St. Peter Nolasco for the redemption of Christian slaves from Turkish hands, chose "Sisters of Mercy." She applied to the Archbishop for sanction as a religious community.

For some time he demurred. The organization had many critics, most of whom considered the women unequal to the tasks they set themselves. Finally Archbishop Murray assented, and Catherine and two companions entered the Presentation Sisters' Convent at George's Hill in Dublin. At this convent, founded by Nano Nagle, they entered upon the course which would find them professed Sisters in December of 1831. On this day the Congregation of the Sisters of Mercy was born. Sister Mary Catherine McAuley was named superior and given the now-familiar title of Mother McAuley.

Seven more women were professed the following year. Growth of the new congregation of
Sisters was instantaneous and widespread. Their
work, too, expanded. More children came to be
educated; more homeless girls sought refuge.
Meanwhile the Sisters continued to visit the sick.
When the cholera epidemic struck in 1832, the
young community could volunteer experienced
service. Hundreds perished in Dublin, despite the
tireless nursing of the Mercy Sisters. They ignored
the risk of contagion, to which many Dublin-
ers felt they should not expose themselves, and
plunged into the distasteful labor with courage
and devotion. Not one Sister contracted the
disease.

The aftermath of the epidemic found children
homeless and orphaned, women widowed, and
whole families dispossessed. To aid them, Mother
McAuley planned a charity bazaar. Again the
doubters warned her, but the shrewd foundress
wrote to the Duchess of Kent for assistance.
Gifts from the Duchess and from her charge, the
youthful Princess Victoria, caused great interest
and assured the success of the event.

For more than three years Mother McAuley
worked at drawing up the Rule of the Sisters of
Mercy. The Rule reflected her own ideals and
conduct by advocating attention to duty, piety
and charity in all things. It was submitted to

Rome, and in 1835 sanction was received from Pope Gregory XVI.

Within a few years of the founding of the congregation, there were fourteen convents of the Sisters of Mercy and four hundred Sisters. These statistics minimize the difficulties and setbacks which Mother McAuley faced. Often the victim of abuse by those who misunderstood her purpose or underestimated her ability and determination, she reflected on what a priest had once told her: "Place no trust in any man. Let God alone be your hope."

In November of 1839, Mother McAuley established a Catholic convent in London. This represented a significant breakthrough in Church relations with the English authorities. The Superior's keen insight, sense of humor, administrative acumen, and persuasive judgement virtually assured progress. At the height of this success, she acquired the tubercular cough which had been fatal to her sister and her nieces.

Throughout 1841, Mother McAuley suffered but continued to pursue her role of foundress and Mother Superior. In the fall of the year, travel in the damp weather caused her final attack. By October she was a dying woman but one determined to conclude her affairs in an orderly fashion. She set about organizing the myriad papers and accounts vital to the Mercy Sisterhood. They were in perfect array before her death.

On her death-bed, Mother McAuley spoke to her beloved companions. She counseled them: "Preserve union and peace. Do this and your happiness shall be so great as to cause you wonder."

By this time she was resigned to the fact that her mission was finished, and she embraced the termination of the struggle. "Had I known death could be so sweet," she remarked, "I never would have feared it."

Knowing the end was near, the Mercy Sisters clustered about her bed. With them Mother McAuley recited the prayers for the dying. Even in this moment, her charitable and practical nature revealed itself.

"The Sisters are tired," she said. "Be sure they have a comfortable cup of tea when I am gone."

Death came on November 11, 1841. After lying in state in her own chapel, Mother Mary Catherine McAuley was buried according to her wishes in the small cemetery behind the convent on Lower Baggot Street.

Had she lived a few more years, the foundress might have thrilled to the return of three Mercy nuns from the battlefields of the Crimea. There, serving with Florence Nightingale, two Sisters had given their lives. Now the remaining nuns marched at the head of a detachment of return-

ing English veterans. The hostile British crowd
jeered at the nuns, bringing down the wrath of
the soldiers. When the commanding officer
praised the great service the Mercy Sisters had
performed, the hisses of the crowd turned to
cheers.

Since that day the Sisters of Mercy have
marched into the history of a dozen nations. Or-
phanages, hospitals, homes, schools and colleges
have been entrusted to their care.

As with all societies, the Sisters of Mercy mir-
ror the ideals of their foundress. The charity of
Mother McAuley and her capacity for accom-
plishment live again in the hearts of her thousands
of successors. As they labor among the poor and
indigent, among the seeker and the lost, the Sisters
of Mercy must often recall the words of their
first superior:

> "It is not a disposition to bestow gifts like benevolent
> persons in the world that bespeaks generosity of
> mind for the religious state; it is bestowing ourselves
> most freely and relying with unhesitating confidence
> on the Providence of God."

(1790-1856) father theobald mathew

CHAPTER TEN

"God's host to save me . . . from temptation of vices."

While ecclesiastical and educational reforms had been inaugurated in Ireland arenas, the social sphere still cried out for attention. The majority of the Irish people were poor, landless, leaderless and without hope. Small wonder, then, that they turned to drink as the remedy for their collective misery. Consumption of intoxicating beverages rose steadily in the eighteenth century, particularly in the cities where money was more plentiful than in the country. With the increase in drinking came a rise in crime, particularly crimes of violence. Intemperance added to the wretched condition of the impoverished Irish.

Into this dilemma stepped an unusual, dynamic and gifted Capuchin friar, Father Theobald Mathew. With Daniel O'Connell, the political giant, Father Mathew captured the hearts and minds of his countrymen during this formative century. In an era when communications were still primitive, he reached millions with his message of temperance.

Theobald Mathew was born at Thomastown, near Cashel, in County Tipperary. The date was October 10, 1790, and the woods around the Mathews' castle-like mansion were crisp with leaves and alive with deer. With his wife Anne and his twelve children, James Mathew tended the estate for a cousin, the Earl of Llandaff. In this romantic setting young "Toby" Mathew spent his youth, first as a resident of the castle, and later in a smaller home on the same grounds. He was remembered as a warm, affectionate boy whose love for animals made him dislike hunting and fishing. He loved nothing better than

sponsoring a party for his friends or for poor
youngsters in the area.

When Toby was about ten, he was enrolled
in St. Canice's Academy at Kilkenny, where his
tuition was paid by a wealthy cousin. At seventeen he entered Maynooth Seminary, but his
generosity proved his undoing. A party given
for his classmates violated the institution's stat-
utes, and Toby was dismissed. While his case was
being weighed, he left Maynooth.

The next few years are indistinct, but in 1810
Theobald Mathew joined the Capuchin Order,
and on Easter Sunday, 1813, he was ordained.

His first assignment was in Kilkenny where
the Capuchins administered a small church. Many
hardships plagued these Franciscan friars because
of the forthright stand they had taken on political
issues and because of the new and more rigid
ecclesiastical discipline. Restrictions were placed
upon their mendicant activities and even upon
their spiritual conduct. Father Mathew was once
forbidden to hear confessions because of some in-
fraction of liturgical privileges. It was a severe
penance for a young priest, and although it was
countermanded soon after, it gave him a foretaste
of the trials which would eventually face him.

From Kilkenny, Father Mathew was transferred to a tiny chapel in Blackamoor Lane,
County Cork. For twenty-four years he lived as

a parish priest, but this simple post could not mask his abilities. Renting vacant rooms and lofts, he began schools for young people, offering religion, standard academic subjects, and, for girls, sewing and housework. After ten years at Blackamoor Lane, he had an enrollment of five hundred students. Father Mathew was renowned as a preacher and as a confessor. While his voice was but average and his manner lacked oratorical polish, his talks had a sincerity and devotional quality which made him extraordinarily effective. Many Protestants came to the crowded chapel to hear him, and eventually plans for a new church had to be set in motion.

The next few years found Father Mathew succeeding his deceased pastor, gathering funds for the new church, securing cemetery space for the poor of Cork, serving heroically during the cholera epidemic, and at all times caring for the unfortunate.

"Every time I see a barefoot child in the street," he said, "I seem to see Jesus Christ Himself."

An exasperated servant in the friary claimed, "If the streets of Cork were paved with gold, and if Father Mathew had entire control over them, there would not be a paving stone left in all Cork by the end of the year."

In 1822, although ordained less than ten years, Father Mathew was chosen as Provincial of the

Capuchins of Ireland, a post he held for the ensuing twenty-nine years.

During his ministry, the young Capuchin came in daily contact with the evils of drink. He saw families destroyed, homes forfeited, crimes accumulating. Protestant clergymen and laity were much more active than Catholics in alleviating this disease. In Cork, an eccentric, insistent Quaker merchant named William Martin was one of the chief opponents of drinking. In his loosely organized temperance group he numbered some Catholics, but subtle proselytizing by a careless minister member began to drive them out. No real temperance movement existed, and William Martin knew that in order to create an effective organization he would need the aid of an influential Catholic priest. He appealed to his friend, Father Mathew, for assistance.

As they walked arm in arm through the streets of Cork, Martin begged the Capuchin, "O Theobald Mathew, if thou but wouldst take the cause in hand! Thou couldst do so much good to these poor creatures."

After attending a lecture conducted by Martin, Father Mathew agreed to consider the matter and promised to announce his decision at a meeting to be held a month later at Blackamoor Lane school. There was a large audience on that April evening, 1838, to hear the priest say:

"I feel I am bound as a minister of the Gospel to throw all personal considerations aside and give a helping hand to gentlemen, like Mr. Martin, who have afforded me so excellent an example. . . . After much reflection on the subject, I have come to the conclusion that there is no necessity of intoxicating drinks for anyone in good health. I will be the first to sign my name in the book which is on the table, and I hope we shall soon have it full."

As Father Mathew entered his name in the rolls of those taking a pledge of total abstinence, he exclaimed, "Here goes in the name of God." With these words, a remarkable crusade was launched.

As president of the new society, the Capuchin traveled about Cork, holding three meetings a week and preaching at all of them. From distant counties men and women journeyed to Cork, often on foot, to hear his words and to take the pledge.

Candidates who came forth at the meetings repeated these words after Father Mathew:

"I promise, with the Divine assistance, to abstain from all intoxicating liquors and to prevent as much as possible, by advice and example, intemperance in others."

After this they were blessed and they signed the book as lifetime members. Cards or medals were distributed free or for a small sum. Both copper and silver medals were used, the latter usually reserved for priests or dignitaries. Members were requested to refrain, as members, from religious and political discussions.

Within three months, 25,000 had taken the pledge. The number grew to 131,000 in five months and 200,000 in nine months. By the time two years had passed, membership was in the millions.

Father Mathew's fame spread, and soon he was forced to accept invitations to preach in other dioceses. Eighty thousand signed up in Waterford, thousands more in Galway. In Dublin, a rain-soaked audience produced 4600 candidates in a single evening and 700,000 before his mission there was concluded. All over Ireland the Capuchin traveled at an exhausting pace. Along the route his carriage made myriad stops to pledge people at crossroads, villages, rural lanes. Both Catholics and Protestants joined the Total Abstinence Movement, giving Father Mathew a vain hope of unity through temperance. Always careful to keep partisan religion out of his movement, Father Mathew drew members from all quarters in Ireland. Crime decreased, rioting at festive occasions declined, and the government officials in Ireland and England were happy to give Father Mathew a large share of the credit.

The Apostle of Temperance was ever wary of

any political affiliation. Since his following was large and loyal, leaders such as Daniel O'Connell attempted to enlist his endorsement. Father Mathew was adamant, however, about the purpose of his crusade.

"There is nothing political amongst us," he said. "Whoever wants politics must go elsewhere."

This stand earned him some enemies. And there were critics with other grievances. Some insinuated that he was profiting from the society, whereas he was actually far in debt. A number of prominent Catholics argued that he was too liberal with Protestants. Then there were the distillers, the tavern owners, and the moderate drinkers who spread rumors about the priest's personal sincerity.

These were the exceptions. Most of Ireland flocked to Father Mathew as pilgrims to a source of refreshment and light. They gave him little rest, even when he was at home in Cork. People sought advice, confession, financial help and cures for their illnesses. Despite Father Mathew's repeated protestations, men and women in ill health continued to circulate the falsehood that he was able to heal the sick.

Having traveled Ireland north and south, east and west, Father Mathew turned to Scotland and England. Most of his candidates were Irish, but the native English received him well. The newspapers wrote kindly of his activities, and he was welcomed in the highest strata of society. In London alone, seventy thousand signed his bulging roster. In Parliament, there were some mutterings about the influence of this Irish priest, but these and the few hecklers at meetings did not deter Father Mathew.

Famous men like Thackeray and Carlyle attended the Capuchin's meetings and left with a favorable impression. They saw him as a strong, forceful preacher, a thorough gentleman, robust and masculine and with the great gift of motivating the weak and the distressed.

But trouble lay ahead. First came financial difficulties brought about by costs of the campaign—travel, medals, staff salaries, printing, free Bibles, postage, rentals, even band instruments and uniforms. Added to this were the countless personal donations made by Father Mathew to the poor and needy. Friends offered some help, but it was never sufficient. A fund-raising banquet failed, and an expected legacy did not materialize. To the end of his life Father Mathew remained in debt, paying what he could, when he could. Part of the problem stemmed from the nature of the movement, but the principal flaw lay in Father Mathew's generosity and poor business sense.

Another blow fell when the Great Famine crushed Ireland. Once again Father Mathew was active in visiting the sick, feeding the hungry, writing to government officials, preaching against profiteering. Typhoid and starvation took 300,-000 lives by the end of 1846. In the wake of this disaster came the deterioration of the Total Abstinence Society. Despair yielded to temptation, and thousands turned their backs on the pledge.

Political and ecclesiastical snubs crowned the years of disappointment. Although the clergy proposed and supported Father Mathew for Bishop of Cork, the vacant see was given to another. The Young Ireland Party castigated the Capuchin because he refused to align his cause with their militant program.

Burdened by these cares, Father Mathew suffered a stroke which partially paralyzed him. Recovery was rapid, but he was a changed man in appearance and in stamina. Still he pursued his apostolate, making plans to reorganize the society. When this was scarcely underway, he suddenly decided to cross the Atlantic to visit the Irish in America. There were many teetotalers there, including the President, Zachary Taylor, and the Vice President, Millard Fillmore. Other famous Americans, such as journalist Horace Greeley and William Lloyd Garrison, the fiery abolitionist, had taken the total abstinence pledge.

The ocean journey was long and difficult, and the ailing priest spent hours in steerage hearing confessions of Irish immigrants. When he arrived in New York he was tired, but the splendid reception buoyed his spirits. City Hall was made available to him for meetings. Here he greeted the Irish-Americans, administered the pledge, or just chatted with them about their homes in Ireland.

From New York Father Mathew traveled to Boston where an Abolitionist delegation requested him to join them in a public display of unity. Although favoring the anti-slavery movement, Father Mathew felt that one crusade at a time was sufficient, so he refused the offer, thus making an enemy of Garrison.

In November of the same year, 1849, Father Mathew was stricken with paralysis again. After two weeks' rest, he toured Philadelphia and Washington. In the national capital, the Senate and House passed resolutions honoring him, and President Zachary Taylor held a formal dinner for him.

From here Father Mathew dropped south, swinging westward from the Atlantic to the Mississippi, covering Virginia, the Carolinas, Georgia and Alabama. His charm and conviction melted prejudice and multiplied his many friends. At New Orleans he conducted one of his most successful campaigns. Then he went up the Mississippi to Natchez, to Vicksburg, along the Arkansas to Little Rock, where the delighted bishop offered him a home in his diocese. Here illness caused him to rest once more.

Father Mathew visited twenty-three states, addressed meetings in more than 300 cities and towns, and gave the pledge to 600,000 persons. Only the current crisis on the Plains prevented him from preaching temperance to the Indian tribes.

Although ill throughout his two and one-half years in America, he reached many hearts and won admirers among all races and creeds. He never forgot his vocation. Once when he was introduced "not as a Roman Catholic priest but as a preacher of temperance," he objected strongly.

> "I am proud, justly proud, of being a humble servant in that holy Church which has done so much for the glory of God and the civilization of mankind, which has stood bravely in the van unchanged from age to age, which has outlived, and shall outlive, both calumny and oppression."

On December 6, 1851, Father Mathew arrived back in Cork after a month's sea voyage. His friends, worried about his health, helped him elude the huge delegation which waited on him. He was a broken man. The society he founded was floundering and his work slipping away from him. His determination to turn the tide was checked by doctor's order to refrain from any labor. The weary priest resigned his office as Provincial and his duties as superior of two Cork convents. He felt obliged to decline an appointment as Vicar Apostolic of Jamaica.

Father Mathew's inability to roam about did not stop people from coming to him with their problems. Gradually he began to do more speaking, some traveling, and some new administrations of the pledge.

To conserve his ebbing strength, friends collected enough money to send him to Madeira in 1854. After a year's absence, he returned with a false vigor which soon deserted him in the resumption of activities. He collapsed and was taken to his brother's house, a dying man. Not wishing to cause inconvenience, he had himself removed to a friend's seaside cottage at Cobh.

Late in November of 1856, he suffered another stroke which left him paralyzed and speechless. Communication was accomplished by touches and almost imperceptible expressions. Even these ceased on the Feast of the Immaculate Conception, 1856, when the sixty-seven-year-old priest mercifully died.

Clad in the Capuchin habit, he lay in state before the altar of Holy Trinity Church which he had helped erect. Thousands passed to pay their final respects and then followed the coffin to St. Joseph's Cemetery.

After the loss of its champion, the Total Abstinence Society declined rapidly. Its interdenominational character began to work against it, as did social and political conditions. Yet it was not a complete failure. Father Mathew had brought the story of the evils of drink to millions of listeners and had banished forever the image of the drunkard as a jolly companion. He also gave impetus to later temperance movements, such as the Pioneer Total Abstinence Association of the Sacred Heart founded by Jesuit Father James A. Cullen, who gave full credit to the inspiration of Father Mathew.

Perhaps one Puritan woman summed up best the character of this unique individual:

"He has wiped more tears from the face of women than any other being on the globe but the Lord Jesus, and thousands of lisping children will bless the Providence that gave them an existence in the same age."

(1856-1925) matt talbot

CHAPTER ELEVEN

"Alone and in a multitude . . ."

Sanctity is not the province of the past nor the exclusive privilege of clerical life. Throughout history many laymen have achieved lives marked by holiness. They have learned to do the ordinary things in an extraordinary manner. Among Ireland's lay apostles, none had more of an impact on his time than Matt Talbot, who died less than forty years ago.

At the time of his death, Matt was a slight,

short, balding man, unimpressive and virtually unknown except to a small circle of family and
friends. On Trinity Sunday, 1925, he walked
down Granby Lane, Dublin, toward St. Savior's
Dominican Church, where he planned to attend
the second of many Masses he had scheduled for
the holy day. A short distance from the church,
he collapsed. Seeing him fall, a shopkeeper ran
to him with a glass of water, then murmured,
"My poor fellow, you are going to heaven."
With a final glance about him, Matt Talbot fulfilled that prediction. A passing stranger blessed
the inert form with a wooden crucifix, and a
priest was summoned to read the prayers for the
dead.

When attendants at the near-by hospital exam-
ined the corpse, they made the discovery which
set thousands of people investigating the mystery
of Matt Talbot. About the dead man's waist
were twined chains, cutting into the flesh and
covered with medals. Smaller chains were about
his arms and legs. Who was this man, they won-
dered? Why did he wear these unique symbols
of penance? The answers to these questions revealed a simple man living a simple life in communion with God.

On May 2, 1856, Matthew Talbot was born
in Dublin, the son of a strict, pious father, who
had a supervisory position at the Dublin Port and

Docks Board. Mrs. Talbot, mother to eight boys and four girls, was a saintly woman who filled Matt's life with love. All of her sons, except Matt and John, died young.

Ireland was again in ferment, and Matt Talbot was to live through some of the nation's most terrible days. Strangely, he paid little attention to the battles and the bulletins. He was listening to another voice, hearing other words. A few years before Matt's birth, Daniel O'Connell, the champion of Irish-Catholic emancipation, died, and the Great Famine swept away entire families while sending thousands of immigrants across the Atlantic. During the lifetime of Matt Talbot, the world witnessed the rise and fall of Parnell, the gallant struggles of the Fenians and the Sinn Fein, the Labor Troubles, the tragic Rising of 1916, the First World War. It witnessed miracles, too, particularly the Apparition at Knock, when the Blessed Virgin, St. Joseph and St. John the Evangelist appeared to numerous villagers in this small County Mayo town.

Until he was twelve, Matt attended Christian School in North Richmond. Scholastically, he made little impression, but the teachers recalled him as a lively, pleasant chap, somewhat prone to truancy. Employment as a messenger boy for a wine merchant followed, and here Matt's troubles began.

Along with many other employees, young and old, Matt would sample the owner's stock. Soon he drank regularly, although it never hampered him in his duties. One evening he came home intoxicated and received a sound thrashing from his father, who, the next day, caused him to be transferred to Ports and Docks. This was from the frying pan into the fire or, more explicitly, from wine to whiskey.

By the time he was seventeen and a bricklayer's apprentice, Matt was an habitual drunkard. Evenings and weekends he could be found at his favorite pub, drinking, talking, treating his companions. His meager wages disappeared in this fashion. He took to depositing his paycheck with the bartender and then drinking until it was exhausted. Although he continued to attend Sunday Mass, he remained away from the Sacraments, scandalizing his mother and sisters. His brothers, with one exception, shared his fondness for liquor. Though Matt drank to excess and carelessly cursed, his words and actions were never coarse or lewd. In other aspects of his conduct, he was decent and prudent.

The one vice, however, seemed sufficient to destroy him. When he ran out of drinking money, he would pawn his boots and other belongings. One evening he even helped some companions steal the fiddle of an itinerant musician and trade it for cash. The fiddler wept at the loss of his livelihood, creating such a sense of guilt in Matt that he searched the streets of Dublin for years afterward, hoping to make amends to the wronged man. Still he persisted in his profligate ways.

One day, when he was twenty-eight, his mother's prayers were answered. Matt concluded a week-long spree, broke and with his thirst still unfulfilled. With a brother, Phillip, he waited outside his favorite bar, expecting his friends to buy him a drink, as he had so often done for them. All passed him by, some even crossing the street to avoid him. In this disavowal, Matt Talbot got a glimpse of himself and the shallow existence he enjoyed. Sober and pensive, he returned home and went to his room to think. When he emerged, he announced that he would "take the pledge" to refrain from drinking. Encouraged by his mother to invoke God's help, Matt replied firmly, "I go in the name of God."

At near-by Cloncliffe College he took a preliminary pledge for three months, later extending it to six months and then for life. While at the college he went to confession and, at 5 A.M. the next morning, received Holy Communion for the first time in years.

The change was complete and permanent, but the struggle was not easy. Temptations to drink assailed him, so he had to avoid his former companions and their familiar haunts. Many times he felt he could not endure the privation, but his mother urged him to continue. To give himself spiritual strength, he attended early Mass before work and then, after closing, he made a visit to church before returning home.

This was the beginning of a dedicated life filled with devotion and sacrifice.

Matt retired each evening about 10:30, sleeping on bare planks with a wooden pillow. A statue of the Madonna was in his right hand, clasped over his heart. On cold nights he would be covered with a sack; otherwise, his rude cot sufficed. At 2 A.M. the alarm woke him. He would kneel erect by his bed, often with arms outstretched, and pray for an hour or two. His mother, who shared the room with him during much of this period, often heard him in conversational tones, as if speaking familiarly with the Blessed Virgin. Matt rarely discussed these prayers, except to remark that no one realized how good the Blessed Mother was to him. On occasion he would chant hymns in a low voice.

At 4 A.M., Matt would dress and then pray for an hour before going to church. Until the church doors opened, he would kneel on the stone steps. Policemen making their early morning rounds became used to seeing the silent figure

lost in prayer. At 5:30 he entered the church,
made the Stations of the Cross, and attended the
6:15 Mass at which he received Holy Communion. He used no missal but followed the Mass
closely, praying all the while, always kneeling up-
right in his pew. In order to make this more of a
penance, Matt slit his trousers along the seams so
that his knees would come in contact with the
hard floor. When standing, the slits were not
noticeable.

After Mass, Matt returned home for a small
breakfast and then went to work, making a brief
visit to church on his way. In order to continue
to attend early Mass, Matt changed jobs, taking
a position in a lumber yard where he remained
the rest of his life. His tasks consisted of filling
orders, loading wagons and similar chores. Whenever he had a rest period, he repaired to the little
shack in the yard which became known as
"Matt's Office." Here he prayed until another
wagon arrived. His lunch was small, usually consisting of a nauseous mixture of tea and cocoa.
At 6 P.M. he changed clothes, left the lumber
yard, stopped by church before supper (which
he ate on his knees), and then spent the evening
in prayer or reading until it was time to retire.
Several nights a week he might attend meetings
of the various spiritual societies to which he be-
longed.

During the first years of his "conversion," he moved away from home because his brothers refused to stop drinking. When his father died in 1899, he moved back with his mother. Once he considered marriage, but after making a novena decided against it.

Everything in his life was directed toward Christ. He even wore pins crossed upon his sleeve as a constant, homely reminder of the crucifixion. On Sundays he attended every Mass he could work in, starting with the earliest and lasting until 2 P.M., when he had his first meal. The rest of the day was spent in prayer or reading.

Matt Talbot's diet was a strict one, consisting of cocoa and bread for breakfast, a mixture of tea and cocoa and some bread for lunch, and a light evening meal. He observed a Black Fast (two meals, no meat, butter or milk) during Lent, the month of June, every Friday, Saturday and the vigils of feast days.

The chains on his body and the wooden bed were not Matt's only mortifications. He even gave up smoking, one of his few pleasures. All of these things were done under the direction of a spiritual counselor, and they were done without fanfare or complaint.

Matt's solace was in his faith. When a friend lamented her own loneliness, Matt rebuked her gently. "Lonely? How can you be lonely with Christ in the Tabernacle?"

Temptations continued to plague Matt periodically. One morning at Mass he found himself unable to stand up to go to Holy Communion. Some physical force held him down. He left to go to Mass in another church, but the same sensation overcame him. At a third church he knelt in the rear and surrendered himself to the protection of the Blessed Virgin and her Divine Son. Only then was he able to walk to the communion rail.

From his reading about the saints, Matt Talbot drew inspiration. He seemed almost on familiar terms with them, referring often to the female saints as "great girls." Frequently, he would jot down on scraps of paper little thoughts that appealed to him—thoughts about sin and penance and love and grace—passages which seemed to be catechism answers, dates of Church councils or of saints' deaths. Matt's own library was supplemented by spiritual reading borrowed from friends.

Matt was no wild-eyed fanatic. Although his clothes were poor, he was invariably clean and neat. Money he might have spent on himself was given away, usually to the church. He supported foreign missions and aided seminarians. His friends found him willing to assist them in any

need except drinking. During his mother's lifetime, he gave her a large share of his wages and
used the remainder, except for a few shillings, for
charity. His charity included prayer, for he was
often asked to pray for people's intentions. One
priest remarked that Matt never prayed for anything for him that was not granted.

Whenever he could, Matt tried to influence
others to live better lives. Though not preachy or
prying, he left no doubt where he stood on moral
issues. When men cursed in his presence, he lifted
his hat reverently. When they repeated dirty
stories, he reminded them that Christ was listening. When they came to him for advice, he counseled them wisely. With little children he was
particularly friendly. Two little girls who lived
near the lumber yard often shared his lunch hour.
To them he'd recount the lives of the saints in
story fashion, pointing out the examples, drama-
tizing the miracles.

With his superiors, Matt Talbot was respectful
but frank. Never late or absent from work, he
refused overtime pay on the grounds that he had
many free hours during the day. Once he argued
with the foreman, and, although justified in his
own mind, he still apologized for the injury he
had done him. During the periodic strikes of the
era, Matt sympathized with the workers but did
not march with them. Instead, he remained away

from work as they did but spent the time in prayer for them and their families. His companions forced him to accept the strike pay which he felt he hadn't earned. This was as close as he got to the political issues of the day. Unless they had a moral implication or unless they touched him personally, he quietly ignored them.

When Matt's mother died in 1915, his pattern changed little. One of his sisters prepared his evening meal and tried to make him as comfortable as he would permit. Until a few years before his death, he enjoyed good health. A heart attack sent him to the hospital twice in 1923. Before entering the hospital, he removed the chains from his body to forestall comment. Responding to the kind treatment of the nuns at Mater Misericordiae Hospital, he was dismissed after a lengthy stay. His first visit was to the hospital chapel. He explained to the nuns that he had thanked them and the doctors and was now thanking the Great Healer.

For some months he lived on National Health Insurance Act payments. His suffering was intense, and he had to moderate his diet and conduct slightly. Instead of fasting throughout Sunday morning, for example, he would eat after early Mass and then return to church.

When he was well, Matt resumed his duties at the lumber yard, carrying out his chores and maintaining the spiritual course he had pursued for forty years. Death on Trinity Sunday, June 7, 1925, found him still in search of the perfection he sought.

Matt's coffin bore the inscription, "The Servant of God, Matthew Talbot." A limestone Celtic cross marks the grave where visitors come daily to pray. His home and the place of his death are also marked, and pilgrims stop for a momentary ejaculation or a decade of the rosary.

Matt Talbot's canonization cause has been advanced, and many faithful in Ireland and elsewhere are hopeful that recognition will come to the shy, smiling workman who conquered his own weakness and gave strength to thousands who suffered.

(1882-1956) bishop edward j. galvin, s.s.c.

CHAPTER TWELVE

"Christ in the heart of every man who thinks of me"

History's reputation for repeating itself often relies on logic and tradition. The spiritual and personal imprint of St. Patrick, for example, has conditioned the missionary character of Ireland these past 1500 years. Like Patrick, his centuries of disciples became "exiles for Christ," ranging the Old World and the New, baptizing, preaching, suffering.

One of these, Bishop Edward J. Galvin, was a man Patrick would have understood and loved. His counsel to a fellow priest was: "Put St. Patrick in front of you, St. Columban behind you, put your head down and plow away."

This advice came from a man who exchanged his quiet home in Cork's Bride Valley for forty years in China. He endured captivity by bandits, the Japanese and the Communists. He triumphed over flood and famine, disease and war, becoming known as "the most bombed bishop in the world." His legacy to the Christian world is the Columban Fathers, a missionary society now serving North and South America, Ireland, New Zealand, Australia, Japan, Korea, Burma, the Philippines and the Fiji Islands. Like all great enterprises, it had humble beginnings.

Father Galvin, finding his home diocese crowded, looked abroad for his first assignment and spent three years as an assistant pastor in the Brooklyn, New York, parish of a gruff, eccentric but kindly Irish pastor. He loved his work and his eighty-year-old superior, but he was filled with a hunger for the missions. His initial attempts to volunteer were thwarted, but a Tuesday morning visit by the Rev. John M. Fraser changed all that.

Father Fraser, a Canadian, was touring the United States, raising funds for his mission work in China. Impressed and inspired by his conversation with this stranger, Father Galvin begged the missionary to take him with him on his return to the Orient. There were delays while various permissions were secured, but soon Father Galvin was bound for China. From Vancouver he mailed a letter to his mother:

> "I am sorry, dear Mother, to have to write this letter, but God's will be done. Everything is in His hands. Mother, don't grieve, don't cry. God has called and I had to obey.
> I am not going back to Ireland. I am going as a missionary to China. . . .
> God knows my heart is broken, not for myself, but for you whom I love above all the world. . . .
> Mother, you know how this has always been on my mind. But I thought it was a foolish thought, a boyish whim, that it would pass away as I grew older. But it never passed. Never, never, never. . . ."

From Vancouver they sailed to Shanghai and then took a train to Hangchow, where the two priests separated. Father Fraser went to his own vicariate of Ningpo, and Father Galvin remained with Bishop Faveau, the Vincentian who administered West Chekiang. Before leaving, Father Fraser returned to his favorite topic.

"It's no dream," he insisted. "There will be a

day when China will be full of men like you, Ed. Apart from ourselves, there are only four English-speaking priests in all of this vast land. But this will change, and before too long."

Father Galvin reflected on this prophecy as he went about the demanding task of learning the country's language and customs. China was in a state of political and social upheaval, and even the progress of Christianity was unsteady. A succession of anti-clerical governments in Paris had made the education of French missionaries—the backbone of the China missions—extremely difficult. The First World War was to call many of them back to France. Father Galvin began to appreciate the wisdom of Father Fraser's dream as he toured the province, making the rounds of the villages on foot and living like a peasant. In his spare moments, he wrote letters of appeal to the priests and seminarians at Maynooth, Ireland's national seminary.

"More priests," he pleaded. "You get to that wherever you begin. There is a work awaiting English-speaking missionaries that no others can do. I believe Ireland could do wonders among the heathen were she to set herself to the task."

His facile pen described the pitiful state of Chinese existence, but it also paid tribute to their industry, their strong family loyalties, their cheerful patience in times of stress. He blended

humorous tales of his own experiences with re-
marks on the culture, customs, philosophy and
living conditions of his neighbors. But every message was a "trumpet call," as he described it, to
enlist more in the service of China:

> "Pray, my dear friends, that God may send us priests
> to gather in this rich harvest of souls. At every Mass
> I pray for it; I pray that God may send us the sons of
> holy Ireland. It will be a sacrifice to some, but we are
> priests. Our aim in life is to send God's work forward,
> and what of the sacrifice when it is God who asks
> it of us? Ireland never failed when God called."

In December of 1915, two young Maynooth
priests, Father Joseph O'Leary and Father Patrick O'Reilly, heeded the call and met Father
Galvin in Shanghai. Almost immediately they
were on the familiar topic of the Irish mission
movement. The two newcomers urged Father
Galvin to return to Ireland and organize the efforts, but he demurred, feeling himself unknown
and unworthy. After some months, Father
O'Reilly broke the impasse by suggesting a novena of Masses for this intention.

"On the last day of the novena," he proposed,
"we will cut the pages of the Bible, and the verse
at the top of the right-hand page shall be our
guide." Father Galvin agreed and, after nine days
passed, the two men knelt in their quarters and

parted the Old Testament at the Book of Josue.
Silently, they read the text:

> "Behold, I command thee, take courage and be strong.
> Fear not and be not dismayed; because the Lord the
> God is with thee in all things whatsoever thou shalt
> go to."

Father Galvin accepted his "orders" and left
for Ireland as soon as possible. En route he
visited the United States, which he had come to
love. Cardinal Mundelein of Chicago encouraged
him.

"If the idea is from God," the Cardinal remarked, "it will bear fruit; if not, it will come
to nothing."

When he arrived in Ireland, he found things
changed. Many young men were fighting in
Flanders; others, ironically, were languishing in
prison after the Easter Rebellion of 1916. A new
and infectious spirit was abroad in the land.

Father Galvin set to work and discovered that
his letters had made many friends. One of these,
Father John Blowick, a member of the Maynooth staff, was to become the society's first
Superior General. He and other friends supported the proposal Father Galvin presented to
the assembly of Irish bishops that October, 1916.
It suggested that a mission house, or college, under the care and authority of the Irish hierarchy,

be founded to supply priests for work in China. Anxious hours followed, but the project won approval and Father Galvin began immediately the solicitation of men and money that would make the mission a reality.

Ireland was canvassed first. There were difficulties and some reverses, but success was the dominant note. While traveling on one of these campaigns, a companion suggested St. Columcille as the society's patron.

"Ah, no," said Father Galvin deliberately. "When I was out in China, I remember reading about that great man Columbanus. That's the sort of patron we want."

And thus the society was baptized, becoming Saint Columban's Foreign Mission Society. Land and a building were purchased for the seminary at Dalgan Park, Galway, and Father Galvin was now free to raise funds and recruit priests in America. He found both, and in Omaha, Nebraska, he found an American home for the Columbans. At first it was merely a downtown office where the society's monthly magazine, *The Far East*, was inaugurated, but it eventually occupied one of the most beautiful sites along the Missouri River.

Back to Ireland briefly, then, for the departure of the first missionary group. The Columban Fathers now numbered forty, and they had been assigned a mission territory in China. In 1920 Father Galvin led them there.

Where the Han River merges with the Yangtze, there is a triangle of cities—Hankow, Wachang, and the smallest and oldest of the three, Hanyang, which became Father Galvin's diocese. In 1927 this area, encompassing 4,000,000 persons, was named a vicariate, and Father Galvin was consecrated its first bishop. Four Christian Brothers and half a dozen Loretto Sisters arrived to share the Columban burden. Later the Columban Sisters would form an heroic auxiliary.

Hardly had the Columbans settled in Hanyang when disaster threatened. Into the provinces came the Nationalist Chinese Army seeking to suppress the militant warlords. One branch of the army was strongly Communistic, and they organized peasants, laborers and students along Soviet lines whenever they entered a new territory. Strikes, riots, murder and pillage resulted. Then Chiang Kai-shek broke with the Communist elements, and a new internal conflict ensued. Caught in the center of the struggle were the Columban missions, now expanded to include Nancheng.

Father Timothy Leonard was stabbed to death before his altar at Nancheng. His martyrdom was followed by that of Father Cornelius Tierney who died in a Communist prison.

Even Bishop Galvin fell into their hands.

While inspecting a new dispensary at the outlying district of Sientaochen, he, several priests, and
the newly-arrived Columban Sisters were surrounded after a pre-dawn Communist raid. A
Red officer assured them of their safety, so they
left their refuge in the church and moved to the
adjoining catechumenate.

Suddenly the Bishop heard shouts and the
splintering of wood. He rushed out to see the
soldiers despoiling his church. Furious, he
ordered them out and they obeyed. Still, he
feared for the Sisters. Distracting the attention of
a Red sentry, he led the priests and nuns through
a back entrance of the compound. They sprinted
across the open fields and into the woods. While
circling back to Hanyang, they were once nearly
discovered but hid in a patch of young wheat as
the Communist soldiers filed past.

The return to Hanyang unveiled a new problem—the worst flood in sixty years. Two-thirds
of the vicariate was under water. Twelve thousand Chinese had drowned and seventy-five mil-
lion were left homeless or seriously impoverished
by the torrent. Even the Columban residence was
flooded, and, across from it, thousands of refugees
swarmed onto the high ground.

Once more Bishop Galvin and his Columbans
turned a catastrophe into a triumph. Halting
other activities, the Bishop organized priests, Sis-

ters and other volunteer help into full-time relief units. They shared their meager food supply, innoculated the young and old, comforted the sick and helped bury the dead. No one worked harder than Bishop Galvin, who labored eighteen hours a day, crawling into the most disease-ridden huts to relieve pain or confer baptism. When the waters receded and the refugees—nearly 100,000 of them—returned to their villages, they remembered the kindness of the missionaries.

A golden era began for the Columbans, and it was to last a decade. More than 40,000 pagans were adequately instructed and baptized in that period.

"Perhaps one day, who knows," the Bishop mused aloud, "Hanyang may be as Catholic as Ireland. And why not?"

In this busy but peaceful period, the Columban Fathers became better acquainted with their remarkable founder. They found him a man of great courage, perseverance and humility. He demeaned his own efforts and spoke of appearing before God with empty hands.

His own robes were worn and patched, his quarters as simple as any up-country residence. No work was beneath his dignity and no assignment too perilous. He asked of his priests that they share the spirit of poverty and sacrifice that marked the life of Christ.

"The disciple is not above the Master," he would quote. "If you expect anything more than He had, you are a very foolish man."

Another time he exclaimed, "This work is as drab and crude as—Calvary!"

Those who knew him then recall his democratic administration, his unfailing sympathy and his continual good humor. Some nights he would be out among the villagers, entertaining them with stories of Ireland or America. Other nights he would regale his own priests with tales of his early priesthood.

His mother's last illness brought him back to Ireland in 1935 and then back to China where conversions and vocations flourished. His cathedral at Hanyang was completed and Chinese priests and Sisters were added to the growing society. Already the Columban missionaries were moving into the Philippines, Korea and Burma. It seemed too good to last. And it didn't.

In 1937 the Japanese invaded China. Again refugees poured into Hanyang, and Bishop Galvin was given the responsibility of feeding them. Then the war moved closer and the refugees were forced to move to a new safety zone. The Bishop, carrying a crippled boy on his shoulders, led the long procession to safety. He became manager of the new zone, supervising the 300 volunteers who fed, sheltered, clothed and tended the 85,000 dispossessed. The zone and the Bishop fell into Japanese hands.

The Japanese found Bishop Galvin a formidable foe, even in defeat. When the enemy commandant wryly suggested that he might appropriate the cathedral, the Bishop replied:

"You will not need tanks for that. But if you enter it will be over my dead body."

The Japanese abandoned the idea. But things did not improve, particularly after the United States entered the war. As Irish citizens, the Columbans were not imprisoned, but they were watched constantly and harassed.

There were a few amusing incidents: the Japanese discovery of a statue of St. Joseph in the rectory with a small American flag clutched in his hand; the charge that a man was concealed in the convent until a large and embarrassed nun slipped on the oversized shoes which had created this suspicion.

The bombings were quite another thing. Almost every day the American bombers hit Hanyang and the frightened citizens crowded into the cathedral. In June of 1944 everything around the church was blasted, but the cathedral escaped damage.

At last the bombings ceased and the war was over. For the sixty-three-year-old Bishop this meant renewed activity. He toured all of the mission villages, subsisting on a cup of weak Chinese tea in the morning and a cup of coffee in the early afternoon. Only when his day's labors were concluded would he eat his first full meal.

There were a few more good years, much like the thirties. American soldiers visited the Bishop, and he entertained prelates from Ireland and the United States. Then, as Bishop Galvin had predicted, the Communists returned. This time, however, they were not bandit hordes but a highly trained, efficient organization with a set purpose in mind. They had come to stay.

In 1949 the shuffle of their ragged sandals was heard in the streets of Hanyang. The city succumbed without a struggle.

At first there was little interference with mission work. By 1950 that changed, and the Korean War stepped up the Red conquest. Sometimes opposition was liquidated; sometimes it was subtly removed. Communist textbooks were introduced in some schools; other schools were taken over completely. Chinese priests and Sisters were exposed to brainwashing, and all religious were subjected to endless questioning. Mission funds were supervised by the Reds. They tried to starve out the priests. When Bishop Galvin refused to cooperate in any way with the Communists, they seized much of his church property and expelled large numbers of priests and nuns.

Soon there was but a small group of Columbans who closed ranks about their bishop.

"There will be no heroics," he told them. "No one is to invite martyrdom. That would be calling down the wrath of the Reds on our defenseless people. We must make it as difficult as possible for the Reds to dislodge us. The longer we stay, the better prepared will be our Catholics to carry on on their own."

The mental torture continued—daily. Even on Christmas Day, 1951, they were interrogated for hours.

"Only the power of God can deliver us from evil, from Evil Incarnate—for that is what Communism is," he told his companions. "I would advise you to say that great prayer of our own St. Patrick daily."

Together they would chant, as that brave band did 15 centuries before:

Christ with me, Christ before me, Christ behind me, Christ in me. . . .
Christ in the heart of every man who thinks of me. . . .

Another year passed, and now there were but three Columbans left in Hanyang. All were under house arrest, of course, and at the mercy of the Communists. But the Reds were determined that they would be expelled as "criminals" after sentencing by a People's Court and after testimony by Patriotic Catholics.

It took a long time to build the case because Bishop Galvin had prepared his flock for suffering and resistance. They remembered how he cared for them in times of peril.

"When the Japanese came up the river, and we were faced with starvation, what did Mao-Tse-tung do?" the widow Fu asked two Catholic apostates. "The only ones who stayed to take care of the people were Kao-Er-Wen [their name for Bishop Galvin, meaning 'the Exalted and Literary One'], and the priests and Sisters. And now you want me to go to meetings and make accusations against the Church! I will never do it! Get out of here, you pair of villains of bandit ancestry!"

A committee was formed, nevertheless, and the two apostates denounced their bishop. Their reward was ten bowls of rice apiece. The only charge they could bring against Bishop Galvin was that he was proud and that, when people kissed his ring, he slapped them. It was enough. He was found guilty, and within three days he was expelled.

With tears in his eyes, he walked down the worn path past his beloved cathedral for the last time. Raising his hand in benediction, he blessed all of his diocese, commending it to the protection of Our Lord, His Blessed Mother and St. Columban.

A Columban Sister met him in Hong Kong and described him as thin and worn looking, "more like a beggar than anything else."

"But," she added, "he struck everybody by the great dignity, courtesy and air of triumph about him. It was the triumph of the Passion, the victory of the Cross."

As he sailed from China, his hair white and his health broken, he had nothing to show for his forty years there. But he did not feel vanquished. He had seen a handful of missionaries expand to a society numbering more than one thousand priests and Sisters, and he was convinced that a great church would rise from the ruins of China. He told himself he would return.

In Los Angeles, however, his illness was diagnosed as leukemia. Although weary and in pain, he did not stop working but visited bishops across the United States, seeking their assistance in promoting the observance of St. Columban's feast by the entire Church.

By the spring of 1954, he was back in Ireland. For a year and a half he dragged himself between his family home in Cork and the mission headquarters at Navan. When his legs would no longer sustain him, he liked to be driven through the Boyne Valley to Tara or to the Hill of Slane where Patrick had hurled his challenge to a pagan nation.

February of 1956 found him dying at Navan. Bishop Cleary, another veteran of the China missions, visited him and asked, "Will you not promise to look after me and the poor Catholics of Nancheng?"

Softly, perceptively, Bishop Galvin replied, "Yes, I will."

He died the next morning and was buried in a little cemetery at the foot of Tara. Among the mourners were a group of Chinese students who carried scrolls telling of the deeds of "Kao-Er-Wen, the priest who had given his life for China."

China would one day respond. Too much of Bishop Edward J. Galvin remains there for any alien force to subdue. His own epitaph might have been the lines from the Hymn to St. Patrick which he loved to quote:

"And the fire thou shalt kindle will ever burn bright,
  Its heat undiminished, undying the light."

afterword

In the history of Ireland one can see in miniature
the progress of Christianity. Delivered from pa-
ganism by heroic missionaries, the Church enjoyed a long period of dynamic expansion, then
laxity followed by reform, and, finally, persecution and the hard-won fruits of freedom. The
story comes full circle as the Irish continue to
pass on to pagan peoples the faith they were first
bequeathed and then fought to retain.

Many other holy men and women deserve
space within this volume. Saints Kilian, Finnian,
Colman, Aidan, Finnbarr, Flannan, Kevin,
Kieran and countless minor saints have tales of
their own which need telling. Another time, perhaps, for this cycle has run its course.

Since saintly lives are calculated to inspire us, a fitting close might be a "Prayer to the Saints of Ireland" which I first learned from an Irish missal as a prisoner of war in Germany:

PRAYER TO THE SAINTS OF IRELAND

O God, who didst deign to people our land with innumerable saints, and to make it illustrious amongst all the nations of the world for the zeal of its apostles, the fortitude of its martyrs, the constancy of its confessors, and the shining purity of its holy women, give us the grace of devotion to all the Saints of Ireland that we may be inspired by their example to lead lives worthy of the noble traditions which they have handed down from generation unto generation.

Teach us humility in Thy service through our recognition of the sins we have committed and through the sense of our own unworthiness. Help us to realize how far short we fall of those saintly heroes and heroines of our land, who found their joy in patient suffering, who learned in the school of Christ the necessity of self-denial and the duty of reverence, and who sought in penance and mortification a safeguard against temptation and all worldliness.

Thou hast endowed us, O God, with the priceless gift of faith and provided us in abundance with heavenly help to deepen our sanctity and intensify our love; but we have not responded to Thy generosity, as the Saints of Ireland did, and pride in our past glory has often blinded us to dangers and evils of our day. Fill us with the spirit of compunction for our sins and reverence for Thy Law. Vouchsafe to grant us, O merciful God, the grace to place our trust in the Sacred Heart of Jesus, to whom our country is solemnly dedicated, that we may ever advance along that road which led St. Patrick, St. Columcille, St. Brigid, St. Laurence, St. Malachy, Blessed Oliver Plunkett and all the other saints of Ireland, amidst trials and afflictions, poverty and misery, executions and suffering, to the land of peace unending, and to the glory of life everlasting. Through the same Christ, Our Lord. Amen.